A YALE ALBUM

A YALE ALBUM

THE THIRD CENTURY

Selection and Commentary by Richard Benson

Yale University in association with Yale University Press

New Haven and London

Designed by Richard Benson.
Set in Minion and Gill Sans typefaces by Richard Benson.
Printed in Singapore by CS Graphics.

Library of Congress Card Number: 00-104786.
ISBN 0-300-08723-3 (cloth : alk. paper).
A catalogue record for this book is available from the British Library.

The paper in this book meets the guidelines for permanence
and durability of the Committee on Production Guidelines
for Book Longevity of the Council on Library Resources.

10 9 8 7 6 5 4 3 2 1

Contents

Foreword vii

PRESIDENT RICHARD C. LEVIN

I   Old Yale, from the Bicentennial to World War I   1

II   The Construction Era   20

III Life at Yale Between the Wars   36

IV   Life at Yale During World War II   50

V   Postwar Yale   56

VI   Athletics at Yale   68

VII The Turmoil of the Sixties and Seventies   82

VIII The Arts at Yale   98

IX   Life at Yale in the Eighties and Nineties   118

X   Challenges Facing the University   140

XI   Commencement   148

Acknowledgments   166

Photography Credits   168

Foreword

To celebrate the three hundredth anniversary of the founding of Yale, we have commissioned a set of publications that examine and illuminate the University's history and achievements. This book offers a visual record of the past one hundred years as lived on the campus in New Haven.

The twentieth century brought overwhelming change to our society. Much of this change arose from advances in technology that drove revolutions in transportation, communications, and economic activity. Other welcome advances occurred in civil rights, broadening the scope of those encouraged to take full advantage of all that America offers. These changes influenced and strengthened Yale even as the University continued to preserve and pass on the great cultural riches of the past. This attention to past, present, and anticipated future prepared Yale men—and now women—for leadership in every area of society. As we enter Yale's fourth century, we draw students from throughout America and increasingly from around the world. We look forward to expanding the scope and reach of Yale's contributions in the decades ahead.

This book is unashamedly made for Yale's graduates—to reveal for them the University's past century in a sequence of selections that touch upon the period when each was here, while placing each period in the larger context of the University's growth and development. I trust that these photographs, many culled from the archives, will cause graduates to reflect upon why and how the years at Yale change the lives of students forever.

These photographs were chosen by the remarkably talented Richard Benson, Dean of the Yale School of Art. His prose, joined by other Yale voices, accompanies each picture. I hope that you will find as much pleasure as I did in this journey through Yale's third century.

Richard C. Levin
President of the University
and Frederick William Beinecke Professor of Economics

The Yale University Art Gallery owns four paintings by Edward Hicks. One, which we see here, hangs in the alcove just outside President Levin's office. It portrays a genre scene of a peaceful earth, where men and animals live in contentment and no one party eats or kills the other. The picture is perfectly suited to Yale, because this ancient notion of the peaceable kingdom is remarkably close to our subconscious ideal of the University. Academies have often been based on the notion that we can set aside humanity's baser instincts and seek knowledge and enlightenment through discourse and collegial interaction. All of us who teach hold to this ideal, and we recognize that the diverse forms of knowledge that we impart can set down roots in the mind of the student while in school so that, once the student goes out in the world, the tree of understanding can resist the terrible storms of fate and human behavior. Hicks's painting shows men dressed in fine apparel (no women, mind you) and wrapped in a ribbon that promises peace and goodwill to men. The lamb and the lion live together on this bountiful earth, emblems of heaven in the corporeal world. Much of our research, writing, teaching, and scholarly labor go toward supporting this idea, that, in the twentieth century's cynical climate, has been almost embarrassing to admit to.

This beautiful photograph is a platinum print from the Yale Department of Manuscripts and Archives. Platinum printing, a printing process used in the late nineteenth century, showed photographic tone with a silky smoothness reminiscent of deeply dyed silk and polished cotton. This picture, like its printing process, evokes another time, and it is the ideal image of old Yale, just at the point when it slipped into the new and frightening twentieth century. The elms are perfect, the light enchanting, and all the troubles of the external world have been pushed back, so these two young men of means can walk through the Old Campus at an unhurried pace. Yale entered the twentieth century as a small college, having only been named a university in 1887, but the tremendous growth of the past hundred years has transformed it into one of the world's great universities. Most of the elms are

now gone, and the patterned light we find so pleasing in this picture will never be the same again. In the year 2000 students of every color walk with brisk determination from class to class, and the Old Campus is a springboard to the treasures and challenges of the outside world, rather than the idyllic pasture we sense in this charming old photograph.

To record the view below, the photographer is standing on Chapel Street, looking across the southwestern corner of the New Haven Green, toward the College Street side of Yale's campus. The date of the photograph is about 1895, and the large building on the left in this panorama is Osborn Hall.

Osborn was built as a multipurpose building in the late 1880s, but it came down in the 1920s, when Yale's building boom began. There was some talk that Osborn was raised more to satisfy a donor than to serve the University's needs. Whether or not this criticism is true, it was an unusual structure in that the main doorway faced the city and not the University. Osborn's central door and grand entry steps looked out diagonally onto the base of the Green and the cityscape of Chapel Street, and it provided a note of openness between city and school even as it formed a large section of the Old Campus's surrounding wall. By the time the Harkness and Sterling construction binge was over, and Osborn was long gone, the buildings of Yale College were firmly set in the medieval pattern of the walled city within the larger town-

ship. The University literally built walls separating the residential colleges from the mother city of New Haven. This pattern of construction held for the first part of the twentieth century and was broken only during the widespread expansion that took place at Yale after World War II.

4

3

We don't know who the teacher is, but the picture was made in one of the classrooms of Osborn Hall. The professor awaits the coming class, and the subject is probably biology, specifically the response of animal nervous systems—the apparent subject of the quick sketch on the blackboard. This classroom had those old pressed plywood seats with fold-down writing tables that were found in so many educational institutions. This picture is remarkable because it reveals the patina of scuff marks that adorn the seat backs. Most professional photographers would go to great pains to conceal such marks when they made a picture, because few clients want to see a reality that diverges so starkly from the ideal. Students sitting in this room squirmed and wriggled, sometimes with their feet pressed against the back of the chair, sometimes leaning forward surreptitiously to scratch something on the seat back. This scarcely fits our idealization of the student enlarging his mind. We don't consider how hard it was for young men to sit still, much less pay attention to a lecture in a classroom. This photograph gives us graphic evidence of one aspect of the educational struggle.

5

Ralph Henry Gabriel was a Yale undergraduate in the Class of 1913. He photographed extensively during his time in New Haven, and he later donated a small album containing these pictures to Yale. His snapshots portray a rich student life at Yale in the first part of the century. Most of the photographs depict social life at school, with pictures of outings into town, campus pranks, local characters like street vendors and newsboys, and an occasional stern-looking dean sitting in a common room. The relative dearth of pictures of classroom life in the album suggests an image of Yale as all fun and no work. Consider, though, how hard it is to make a good picture of something as nonvisual as classroom study. Yale's fundamental mission is to teach, but the glamour of college life, when students are set free of their childhood homes, is the dominant theme of most pictures we have of the University's past. Gabriel went on to become Sterling Professor of History at Yale, and he taught at the University for many years.

5 The corner of York and Elm streets before the construction of the residential colleges. 6 A selection of pictures from a photo album by Ralph Henry Gabriel, made between 1910 and 1914. Clockwise, from top left: the City Express; Street Mary, the laundry lady, outside Lampson Hall; entrance to Berkeley Oval; a class in Byers Hall; raising Hale; the trophy room at the old Elm Street Gym; Dean F. S. Jones in his study; newsboys at Yale Station.

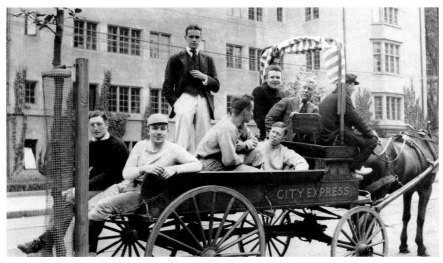

The University held a grand party for its bicentennial in 1901. Connecticut Hall grew rows of folded-paper decorations, the New Haven Green was strung with newfangled electric lights, and Hewitt Quadrangle and its adjacent buildings were constructed as a bicentennial legacy. The Quadrangle abutted University Dining Hall (Commons) on the north, Memorial Hall to the northeast, Woolsey Hall to the east, and Woodbridge Hall—daytime quarters for University Presidents— to the south of Woolsey. Commons was designed to be the sole undergraduate dining hall, and so it remained until the residential colleges were built, each with its own eatery. Memorial Hall has a domed roof, a marvelous rotunda, and walls covered with the incised names of war dead. This multidoored building still serves as crossroads for foot traffic today, and the construction of Science Hill has made it a central point of the campus.

Woodbridge houses the President's and Secretary's offices, and on the second floor is the Yale Corporation room, hung with paintings from the earliest days of Yale and sporting a grand conference table with chairs bearing the name of each Corporation member. It is hard not to be intimidated by this room: fourteen-foot ceilings, pictures spanning two centuries, and a table that extends at least twenty feet. Few undergraduates get to see this room, and most faculty rarely go there except in times of crisis, when a large but confidential meeting place is required, or on the happy occasion when the University bestows some sort of an honor on them. The Corporation Room is the ultimate back room, where decisions of immense effect are made in the most elegant surroundings.

7 *Connecticut Hall in its bicentennial dress.* **8** *A pensive moment in Memorial Hall.* **9** *The Corporation Room in 1989.* **10** *(overleaf) Electric lights on the New Haven Green, celebrating Yale's two hundredth anniversary.*

The following is an excerpt from the 1936 memoirs of Henry Seidel Canby, who received his undergraduate degree from Yale in 1899 and his Ph.D. in 1905. The description of his first contact with Yale is made all the more poignant by the knowledge that he taught at the University for twenty years, before becoming the editor of the *Saturday Review of Literature*.

College Life

From *Alma Mater: The Gothic Age of the American College*

HENRY SEIDEL CANBY

When I first saw the college town it was late September, and I, a somewhat frightened boy from home, was dragging a suit-case full of books across the exciting spaces of the Green. The books were for the final cram before entrance examinations, but that was only a cold trepidation hung somewhere near my heart, which was warmed by very different emotions. Coming from a small city that had never tried to be Athens, my naïve imagination had conceived of a college as an assemblage of Parthenons and cathedrals. What I saw before me that afternoon across the Green would have been disillusioning if I had been realistic. The rather dingy halls, boxes ornamented with pseudo Gothic or Byzantine, were little like my dream, and the beautifully simple relics of the old college of brick Colonial were much too simple to mean anything to my taste tutored in the nineties. But I was far from being realistic, so that in a second of time, between Green and campus, I had dropped, with the easy inconsequentiality of youth, all illusions of architectural grandeur for the real thing, college life. . . .

In all this we of the early nineties and nineteen hundreds were like the students of every fortunate age. They have always made their own world, and their own ways for it, and their own ideals which, whether worldly or unworldly, have had the short-term quality of youth. But the American experience of my generation differed in some important respects. No weight of political or religious responsibility hung over our community, as upon the reforming, revolutionary, or reactionary student bodies of other times and countries. We were naïvely yet arrogantly aware that we belonged to America's golden girls and boys, and had been sent to this pleasant place to work a little and play hard, until our time came. Yet, quite unaware, we were actually in the grip of the time-spirit and the local gods of our country. A philosophy bred of Protestantism and pioneering was pricking us hard. The conventional idea (and ours) of the college as a well-organized country club was quite erroneous. There never was a more strenuous preparation for active life anywhere than in the American college of those days. Our illusion of independence was perfect, but it was an illusion.

And there was a third aspect of this college of the catalogue to which I, as a junior, scorching on my bicycle from a class in English to a student meeting, was almost oblivious but which must be mentioned here. Around the college had grown up in the latter nineteenth century a hap-hazard, ill-balanced collection of professional schools, attended by hard-working meagre creatures with the fun drained out of them, who were looked upon with suspicion by the undergraduates, since few of them had been graduated from our college. These schools plus ourselves made up the university, a circus in which the college was the main ring, with law, theology, medicine, and graduate studies in science or the humanities, for side-shows. The central current of American life, as it was then, flowed through

10

the college, carrying with it the rich spoils of American prosperity, and also respect and affection for this unique institution, which was called, by a strange misapprehension of its strenuous temperament, alma mater. The university, feeding upon this life stream, eventually grew great upon its nourishment, but it was in my day a parasite sucking for its own excellent purposes the blood of the college, or more accurately, of that college life which engendered the loyalty of gift-giving alumni. At the moment when the glamorous college life which dominated us and the college was most vigorous, while we sat at Heublein's drinking our beer and assessing the future in terms of the football team, the leaders of American education were planning to make the sprawling university into a vast system of professional training which now begins to dominate both the college and America.

I went to college at a time when (fortunately for an observer) an old curriculum was still tottering like a rotted house about to fall and in parts already fallen. Before my day college education had been disciplinary. The curriculum was a beautiful unity; neat, harmonious, and inspiring confidence because so many generations had worked out the rules for extracting the maximum of mental discipline from the age-tested subjects of which it was composed. It consisted of the classics, long since emptied of the noble excitements of the Renaissance, but efficiently organized into exercises in grammar and bilinguality; of mathematics; of rhetoric; and of some philosophy, literature, and history: all taught by men who believed in hard work upon hard subjects as the first of the intellectual virtues. It was training rather than an education, yet it had the merit of all systems carried through to a logical conclusion. The professors of that day were taskmasters and looked their part. Some of them still survived in our expansive period, bearded men, a little dusty, whose clothes and faces were as emphatically different from the world's as were the old-time clergymen's. Men sure of themselves, severe, arid, uncompromising, uninventive, uninterested in the constantly new thing which we call life, yet often unexpectedly wise and serene. Or so they seemed in the decay of the age of discipline.

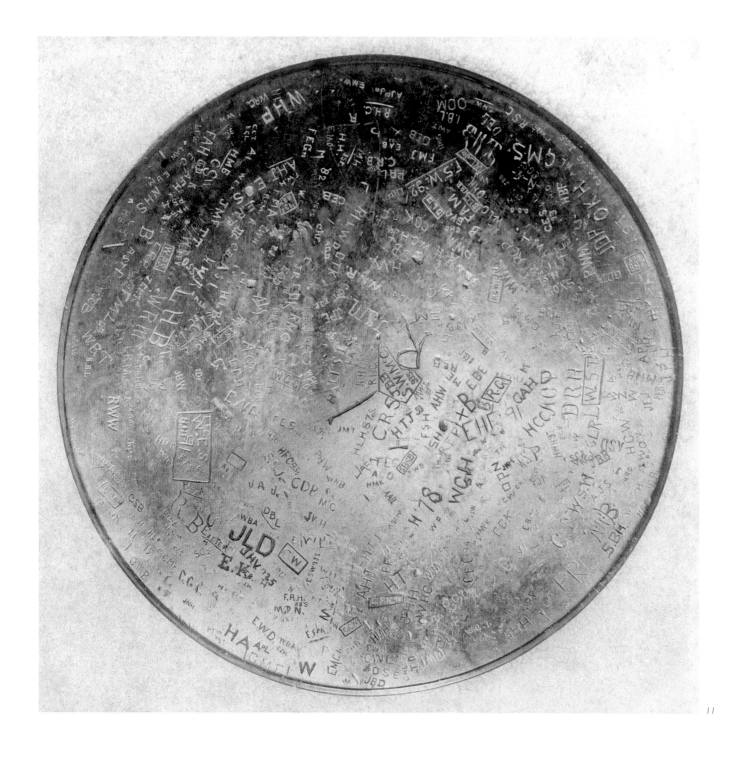

11 *This very tabletop still hangs on the wall at Mory's, in one of the upstairs private dining rooms. Students have carved the tables at Mory's for years, and this one was already old when it was photographed at the end of the nineteenth century.* **12** *A dance held in 1910.* **13** *Calcium Light Night, a fraternity initiation ritual before World War I.*

12

13

14

This building is the Sheffield Chemistry Laboratory, on Prospect Street. Built in 1894, while the road was still dirt, this handsome brick structure originally housed classrooms, laboratories, and ornate residential rooms, which were located on the topmost floor. Yale's archives hold folder after folder of photographs of the University's residential spaces from years past. The rooms have interior furnishings that seem to come from some quintessentially nineteenth-century design manual —wicker chairs and rubber plants, rowing oars, beer steins, books, Oriental rugs, Windsor chairs, and endless Victorian knick-knacks. The building has now been renovated to house computer laboratories, and so, renamed Watson Hall, it goes into its second century dedicated to studies in the dominant technology of the digital age.

14 Fifty-one Prospect Street shortly after it was completed in 1894.
15 A residential room on the top floor of the Sheffield Chemistry Lab. 16 Two students in the Medical School dissecting a cadaver. On the left is A. C. Gilbert, Yale M.D. 1909, who invented the Erector set and founded the A. C. Gilbert Company of New Haven. Hundreds of thousands of Americans were introduced to science and engineering through the creations of Gilbert's company, which produced chemistry kits as well as the Erector set.

15

16

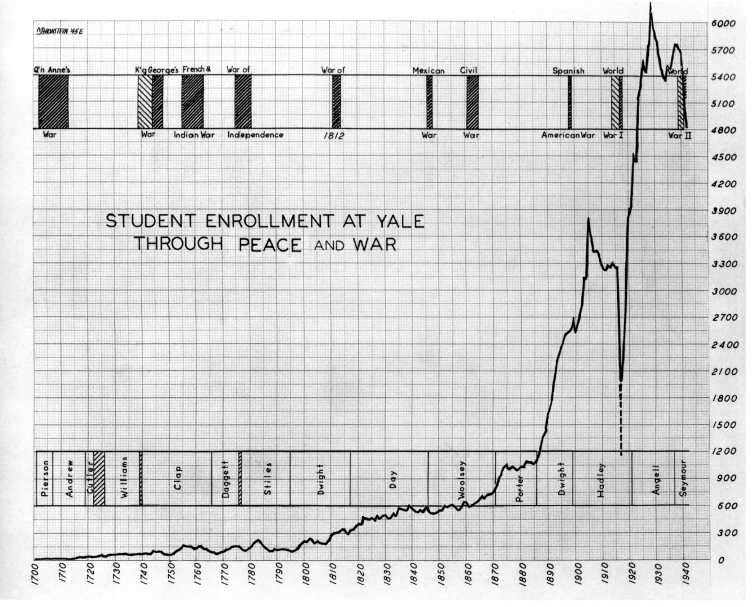

17 Enrollment chart for the first 240 years of Yale's existence. This fascinating diagram, drawn by Martin Aronstein, Yale College Class of 1945,
brings home to the viewer the University's remarkable age. The band
across the top marks the different wars in which the English colonies and
the United States were involved; Yale's early years spanned three
extended periods of wartime before the American Revolution. **18** Artillery
and soldiers in the old athletic cage during World War I.

This remarkable chart shows the student enrollment figures for Yale from its founding in 1701 to the American entry into World War II. Two facts are immediately clear from the chart: that Yale has been growing steadily through its long life, and that patriotism once thrived in this branch of the Ivy League.

The growth of Yale's student population was slow and steady through the first 150 years of its existence, but during the nineteenth century the number of students began to rise more rapidly. Even the Civil War had little effect on enrollment, but in the decades preceding and following the turn of the century the number of students more than doubled. Yale never had more than 1,500 students before 1880, but by 1905 there were 3,600 attending the University. During World War I the numbers fell precipitously, but after the Armistice the count shot up again, and by 1929 more than 6,000 students attended the University.

Why did so many rush to enlist, for both this war and the one that followed in the 1940s? Could it be that at Yale the students saw themselves in national or even international terms? The elegant little New England college had turned into a world-famous center of education, and if this new role was to be fulfilled, perhaps actions outside the shaded quadrangles could no longer be ignored.

World War I mobilized Yale. As soon as the United States entered the war, after it was well along in Europe, the campus literally turned into a military training facility. Artillery appeared at the athletic fields, and many students marched in uniform and served the conflicting gods of higher education and patriotic fervor. There even were directives from the administration that faculty members should be careful to follow orders from students holding higher military rank. It is one thing to have large guns available for study and training purposes, quite another to actually fire them, yet even this happened at Yale. Above, a crowd of sailors and Panama-hatted civilians watch the guns go off outside the walls of Yale's newly built athletic bowl. One of these guns remained at Yale for years after the war, standing in front of the ROTC building at 51 Prospect Street. Once it even underwent the indignity of being painted pink. Finally, in the Vietnam War era, the old artillery piece disappeared.

19 *Members of the Yale* ROTC *firing artillery pieces during Commencement week, June 1917.* **20** ROTC *exercises on the Old Campus during World War I.*

II The Construction Era

Three gifts precipitated a huge building boom at Yale during the first part of the century. One, from Mrs P. W. Whitney, her son John Hay Whitney, and her daughter Joan Payson, in memory of her late husband, underwrote the construction of the Payne Whitney Gymnasium. A second was from John W. Sterling, who made Yale his primary legatee and whose immense donation to the University led to the creation of the Sterling Memorial Library, the Sterling Law School, the Sterling Chemistry Laboratory, and many other buildings, as well as endowed professorships. The third, from Edward S. Harkness, led to the building of the residential college system at Yale. This gift was offered to Yale in 1928, but a faculty committee turned it down. Harkness made a similar offer to Harvard, whose President immediately accepted it. Yale belatedly asked Harkness for the gift, and finally received it in 1930.

Adoption of the residential college system was a turning point for Yale because it allowed the College to evolve into a large university while retaining the intimacy of small scale. The Harkness gift created nine of the ten planned colleges. Silliman, the bequest of F. W. Vanderbilt, followed shortly thereafter, and thirty years later Ezra Stiles and Morse were added to bring the total to twelve.

The following text is adapted from the Freshman Address of 1983, delivered by President A. Bartlett Giamatti, who describes the relation of the residential colleges to the broad requirements of education.

From the Freshman Address
A. BARTLETT GIAMATTI

A liberal education seeks no reward beyond itself. It presumes no subsequent advantage or skill. It portends no practicality save to shape the capacities to think clearly, to express oneself precisely, and to reason humanely and creatively.

A liberal education is meant to instill a love of learning, and a love of the pursuit of learning, for its own sake. How also to promote a sensitive regard for the common life of others is the grand challenge. Every college devoted to encouraging the liberal education of the individual and a civilized responsibility for the rights and needs of others has therefore faced the question: how to connect how we learn and how we live? How to affiliate the intellectual pursuit of learning and the humane particularities of living?

Yale's answer to the question of how best to connect living and learning is the residential college system, formally inaugurated on September 25, 1933. My conviction, stemming from experience that began upon entering a residential college precisely halfway through the fifty-year period we celebrate, is that the residential colleges, since their founding, have helped shape and focus the education of Yale undergraduates and thus provide an opportunity for combining learning and living unparalleled in this country.

The residential colleges are manageable, intelligible communities within the complex structures of Yale College and the University. Little that is indigenous to the wider University, in terms of human activity, results of intellectual pursuit, or spirited exchange, is foreign to the colleges because the colleges are designed, in addition to student life, for the intermingling of faculty and students. Yet the colleges are not simply miniaturizations of the wider worlds of Yale. Their success stems from their openness to the issues and people from the world at large as well as from their character as residences where a student may sink some roots, find a home and extended family, and shape him or herself. For all the fluctuations in curriculum or programmatic requirement, for all the necessary and desirable differences induced by architecture, tradition, location, and emphases by successive Masters, Fellows, and students, the colleges have responded to the constant educational aims of Yale and are now an essential component of that educational mission.

This description of the role of the residential colleges collapses a great deal of history and contains some of the ideal that must draw us on. The story of how the colleges came to be is a fascinating one, and through it all run two dominant strands. The first is the excitement generated by planning a new venture with such ancient roots—that is, the stimulation provided by adapting to American education and an American institution already over two hundred years old, a system inspired by the colleges of Oxford and Cambridge. To adapt the English residential features, esprit, and sense of individuality without their traditions of administrative and academic autonomy tested the Yale planners wherein the American gift for adaptation and innovation was best fitted to respond. . . .

Giamatti makes the point—all too often forgotten—that the colleges are not simply brick and stone but instead must be viable academic entities. The developmental impulse that produced them made no provision for this, but one of Yale's most illustrious alumni, remembering his time at Oxford, made a gift to Yale in 1952, that has had tremendous lasting effect on the University.

Mr. Paul Mellon made, through the Old Dominion Foundation, a truly seminal gift that changed the nature of undergraduate Yale. That gift supported then and now Directed Studies, the Scholar of the House Program, and teaching in the residential colleges. Then the courses were discussion groups in a regular subject, for sophomore residents in a given college, taught by a fellow of the college. Half a generation later, in 1968, this essential step was built upon when the faculty accepted the recommendation of a committee chaired by Professor John Hall, then Master of Morse College. The program of residential college seminars was born, intended to supplement the regular curriculum with new courses that would gradually supplant the college-based discussion courses.

Students initially were assigned to the various residential colleges according to the Masters' wishes. In the 1950s the University administration shifted to a lottery for the assignments to the colleges. By making this change Yale has developed a residential-college assignment system that avoids becoming a hotbed of competition and elitist preference. There is no belief that such and such a college is the *best* one to belong to, and disruptive patterns of self-centered smugness about the residences have been avoided.

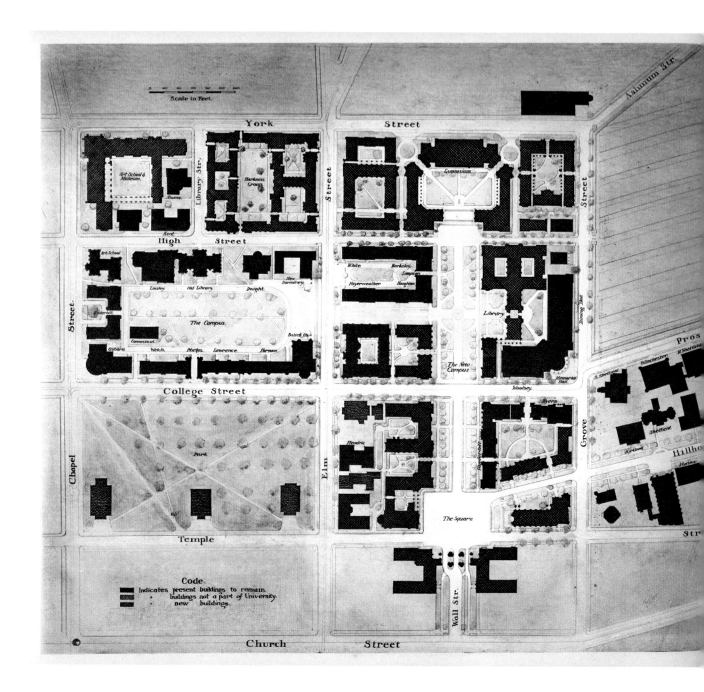

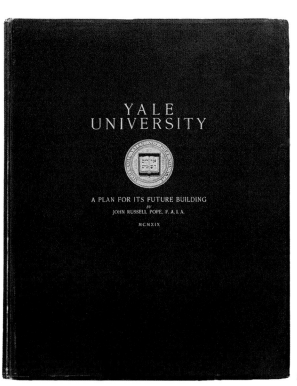

The Pope Plan, sponsored by Mabel Brady Garvan, was commissioned and published in this elegant volume as a gift to the University in 1919. John Russell Pope, a society architect, made a plan for Yale that created a new University based upon the ancient patterns of the great English schools of Oxford and Cambridge. He envisioned pointed arches, intricate masonry, leaded windows, and serene grounds that would form the ideal isolated site for higher education and the elevated culture that it was thought to require. Pope's book was offered as guidance to the Yale Corporation in planning future development of the University. Much of Pope's plan was realized, to the chagrin of some but the pleasure of many. The mock Gothic structures of Yale have weathered a few generations of criticism, and as we enter the new century, they have gained some genuine age. Our University life is unimaginable without these remarkable buildings, and even today we tread carefully when considering alterations to the campus.

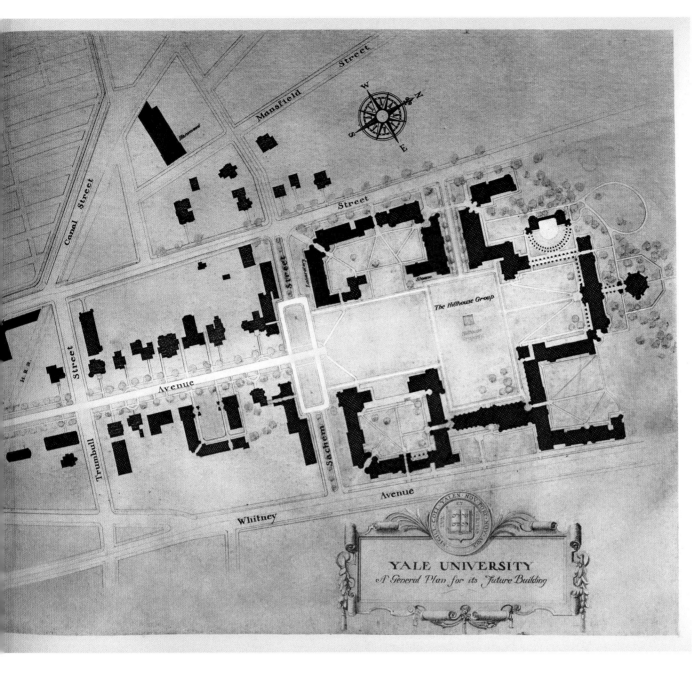

22

21–22 Yale University: A Plan for Its Future Building, *by John Russell Pope. Printed in 1919 at the Cheltenham Press, with drawings by O. R. Eggers, reproduced in hand photogravure. Published in an edition of 250 copies, this 17-by-21-inch volume was funded by Mabel Brady Garvan, in memory of her father Anthony N. Brady.*

The Pope Plan was based upon the idea of a grand overall scheme for the University's architectural layout. The Old Campus was to be joined by New Campus, which was bounded by York, Grove, Temple, and Elm streets. The proposed library on New Campus was to become the intellectual center for Yale, and the University would be entered through a gateway on Church Street that opened onto a great esplanade created by absorbing and enlarging Wall Street. It is worth noting that this tree-lined avenue ended at the gymnasium rather than the library. Today we get a glimpse of Pope's vision when we stand at College Street and look toward the Sterling Memorial Library; this wonderful open view is only about half the length of the original plan. Pope decided—mercifully—that Hillhouse Avenue should remain essentially intact, but he envisioned a new scientific campus growing out of the end of Hillhouse and extending to Edwards Street. This actually took place, though not with the orderliness that the draftsman's layout projected. Yale did grow to the north and cross Sachem, and today Science Hill and the Divinity School form the northern extension of the University.

23

23 An architect's clay model of Memorial Quadrangle, submitted to the Corporation for its approval. **24** Transporting the largest bell of the Harkness Tower chimes. **25** President John Fitzgerald Kennedy delivering a Commencement address on the occasion of receiving his honorary degree from Yale at the University's 261st commencement in 1962.

When the time came to actually build the new Yale, the administration chose James Gamble Rogers, not John Russell Pope, as the architect. Rogers had already laid out the design for Memorial Quadrangle, proposing Yale's first buildings in the style of the ancient English universities. After World War I, the Quadrangle was the starting point for the transforming construction that Rogers directed. He went on to oversee a remaking of Yale that owed a good deal to Pope's original ideas.

One of the most visible elements of the new design for the University was Harkness Tower, a crenellated monument that stands on High Street, built into what is now Branford College. The tower, and in fact most of Yale's new buildings, were much demeaned by the enlightened architectural community of the thirties. It is rumored that whenever Frank Lloyd Wright visited Yale, he asked to be put up in Branford College's guest suite, because this was the only location in New Haven from which one could not see the tower.

26

These empty windows have the unmistakable look of impending destruction; the shrubs and trees show that the houses have stood for some time, and the group of workmen hold the house wrecker's tools—sledges and shovels—that couldn't possibly be applied to the improvement of these old houses.

This is a scene on Park Street in New Haven, and Pierson College was soon to rise where children once played and housewives tended window boxes of summer flowers. Yale was both the savior and shaper of New Haven in the 1930s. The nation was in an economic tailspin, the industrial base had not yet been revitalized by the preparations for World War II, and yet the University was providing good solid jobs as it permanently altered the nature of its native city. The complex feelings that this set of circumstances engendered were bound to affect town-gown relations, and they set the stage for the odd antagonism that characterized New Haven's relation with Yale for many years afterward.

Today, entering a new century, all this has changed. These houses have long been forgotten, and the children of their families have probably gone on to raise their offspring elsewhere. New Haven has finally realized that Yale is one of its great assets, second only to its rich and diverse population; the University for its part has come to realize that its life is dependent upon the health of the city of which it is an integral part. In this old photograph the residents of New Haven stood ready to tear it down for the sake of Yale, but in the future the city and the University need to find a way to thrive as a single entity.

26 *Demolition team on Park Street.* **27** *A sample wall built to show the proposed stonework for the residential colleges.* **28** *A wooden form being used in the construction of vaulting in the Sterling Memorial Library.*

27

28

Everywhere we look on campus we see ornate and ancient-looking stonework. Steps that have been cleverly carved to imitate the wear of centuries of footsteps adorn the college entrances, and arches and lintels of stone that purport to hold up doors and ceilings are scattered throughout the James Gamble Rogers buildings. The surprise beneath the stone is that many parts of these Yale buildings are steel framed, and the real substance of the structures is firmly rooted in twentieth-century technology. The great block of the Sterling Memorial Library stacks depends upon steel and rivet work to hold it up, but the nave of the library is actually made of structural stone, in a building technique hundreds of years old. It is hard to know which stone we see is functional, which merely decorative, but it really makes no difference.

29

30

31

32

29 Construction of the steel frame of the central stacks of the Sterling Memorial Library in 1928–29. **30** Sterling's nave, under construction at night. **31** The library's newly restored reference room. **32** The mural by Eugene Savage behind Sterling's main circulation desk.

Hillhouse Mansion (Yale 1868) near where Temple Street stopped.

33

34

35

Fans of Hollywood Westerns might think that a hanging is about to take place place in the picture at left, the gallows-like scaffolding and the dangling ropes awaiting their load. In fact, the scene is the setting of the Peabody Museum's cornerstone on June 18, 1923. The Peabody is made of brick and stone, and so it really does have an inscribed marker set into the walls, recording the date of construction. Many modern buildings, built of steel and concrete, have to start their lives with the much less glamorous symbolic act of a dignitary prying out the first shovelful of dirt.

Except for a few scattered facilities, Old Yale entered the twentieth century bounded by Chapel Street to the south and Sachem Street to the north. Today the University extends well beyond these limits; Yale College sits squarely in the middle, with the Divinity School forming a spiritual head at one end and the School of Medicine handling concerns of the flesh at the other. The northward march across Sachem began in earnest early in the century when the Sloane and

Osborn laboratories were constructed just before World War I and Sterling lab shortly after. With the laying of the Peabody cornerstone, the colonization of Science Hill was off and running. The Yale of the nineteenth century was little, self-contained, and largely at peace with itself. The new University, which was to grow steadily during the next hundred years, was a completely different creature, spread out physically and programmatically in a diversity of pursuits that are dizzying in their breadth.

33 *A mid-nineteenth-century view up Hillhouse Avenue to Sachem's Wood, the Hillhouse mansion.* **34** *The ceremony marking the laying of the cornerstone for the Peabody Museum. Sachem's Wood is visible in the upper right.* **35** *The Peabody under construction, viewed from the current location of the Josiah Willard Gibbs Laboratory.*

The building is only one piece of the puzzle; far more important is what goes into it. The Great Hall, when new, was a bare
and echoing chamber, with exhibition cases along the walls
and a few ancient bones set up in the middle. As the museum
and public interest in paleontology grew, this huge room
became a prototype of natural-history display. The skeletons
were reinstalled beneath a solid ceiling, shutting out the nat-
ural light so painstakingly preserved when the building was
made, because even a brontosaurus looks small compared
with the open sky. The wall to the east became home to one
of the great illustrations of its time: Rudolph Zallinger's
panorama of dinosaur life spanning millions of years. The
fern-leafed trees, riotous flowers, and belching volcanoes
have become embedded in many thousands of minds, for no
one can stand in this space and not be moved by the
immense mural's impact. As with most good art, we cannot
be sure what is real and what is fiction. The world probably
didn't look anything like this all those millennia ago, but after
seeing this picture, our minds cling tenaciously to its dense
and powerful imagery.

36 *The Great Hall of the Peabody Museum shortly after the museum
opened.* **37** *The original Handsome Dan, stuffed and on temporary display at the Peabody.* **38–39** *Two views of the Great Hall today, showing
the mural by Rudolph Zallinger.*

38

39

The creation of the residential colleges required the destruction of many Yale and New Haven buildings. The beautiful old gymnasium on Elm Street had to go to make room for Trumbull College, and Berkeley Oval, a courtyard whose buildings housed generations of Yale students, also had to be torn down to make room for its namesake, Berkeley College. The photograph above shows the oval in the midst of its destruction, with the footings of White and Berkeley halls remaining on the left and the walls of Fayerweather Hall still standing on the right. The white cloud rising in the picture's center probably comes from a last bit of Lampson Hall, at the oval's far end, biting the dust.

In the front of the picture is the round telephone exchange, built about the turn of the century, to house the newfangled invention of Alexander Graham Bell. This picturesque little tower also fell to the wrecker's ball, but it was immortalized in a carved plaque, still visible on the Elm Street wall of Berkeley College. Many years passed before the telephone became an integrated and invisible part of Yale's infrastructure. The invention had not transformed society when the oval was built, so its central station cropped up in this odd building; today the telephone exchange is huge and hidden, and the phones themselves are in virtually every populated room on campus, and on the exterior walls of most Yale buildings. As they become essential and systemic, the technological underpinnings of our society disappear; electrical wires, heating and cooling pipes, telephone switches, and computer servers all move underground into windowless rooms at Yale so that they can do our bidding without disrupting our working spaces.

41

42

In a marvelous little corner of Pierson College, the buildings are whitewashed and the style is plain. This was called the slave quarters for many years after it was built in the thirties. This name is typical of the insensitivity abroad in America before the civil rights movement, although we can imagine that the "slaves" referred to might have been Yale underclassmen. What is interesting about the name, aside from its dated nature, is that it is an example of the illusory history that had to be created for the residential college system to work. Each college came into being with a carefully crafted fictionalized lineage that gave the appearance of murky, ancient tradition. This worked well because the students at Yale change at regular intervals; by the time the second or third class was occupying any given college, the legends were assumed to be old, venerable, even true. Today the traditions of the residential colleges have gone through many generations of students, and so it is hard to believe that the whole affair was created as recently as the 1930s. Yale's residential colleges demonstrate the healthy maturity of a fully designed community, one that was created in much the same way as the modern planned towns that have begun to spring up throughout the United States.

40 *A 1933 view across Elm Street from the roof of Wright Hall, showing the future site of Berkeley College.* **41** *The old gymnasium on Elm Street.* **42** *Pierson College on a rainy day.*

43

The small picture at left perfectly elicits the wonder and disorientation that one inevitably feels when entering a new stage of life. The well-dressed young gent has his suitcase, fedora, and white bucks, so he is certainly of the right class to be at Yale in the twenties, but his upward gaze—probably at the crenellations of Harkness Tower—denotes the new arrival's sense of wonder and unease. In the lower picture the moving truck has pulled up with everyone's trunks, which will be unloaded and make their way into the waiting residence quarters. We can be sure that the slick fellow sitting on a trunk won't be getting his hands dirty moving it but that the mover himself, with rolled up sleeves, muscular arms, and a careful separation from his betters, will do the job of horsing the trunks up to their assigned spaces.

The truck is quite a sight, showing evidence of a brilliant packing technique that manages to get twice as many cases into the bed as one would ever imagine possible. Back in the twenties the well-to-do used trunks, which were carefully packed for shipment on trucks, trains, or ocean liners. Today we all have cars, and the old art of packing has given way to the modern habit of tossing everything into a pile (or a cardboard box at best) and then dumping it into the automobile, which can be depended upon to act as a large and versatile rolling suitcase.

43 An arriving undergraduate having a first look at Yale. 44 Trunks and laundry cases ready to be unloaded on moving day. 45 A scene on Elm Street in late August 1976.

45

This photograph is completely posed. It purports to show spontaneity, in the lighting of the cigarette and the ostensibly casual postures of the young men, but the photographer has worked them very hard to get the figures in the right place and all the planned gestures orchestrated correctly. The picture pleases us because it is perfectly synchronized with the styles of those whom the photograph depicts. The white shoes, carefully combed hair, and swell clothes testify to the class and status of this privileged group, and the self-consciousness of attire and pose matches that of the form of the photograph. These well-dressed young men will go on to run our country—or fight for it—and they will mature to carry on the culture of their parents. Their own children, to be born in the forties and fifties, will institute the dramatic social changes that have made Yale what it is today.

47

This small and dapper man looks as though he is about to be consumed by his books; the table holds a set of white teeth ready to bite him in two, and the disembodied legs and feet give the viewer a hint of how thoroughly the man will be absorbed by the bound volumes. Metaphor aside, the man and the books had a long and intimate life together, for this is William Lyon Phelps, one of Yale's most distinguished professors of literature in the first part of the twentieth century. He taught many hundreds of students in New Haven, then spread his influence even wider through his written and radio reviews of various publications. In the minds of many, Billy

Phelps invented the form of the modern book review. The wonder of the picture is that it implies that the contents of the thousands and thousands of pages in these books could fit into the brain of this man; they are simply extensions of his intelligence, kept conveniently at hand for his ongoing adventures of the mind.

We think of education as based upon books and intellectual study, but in the twentieth century Yale made a strong commitment to forms of learning grounded in physical experience. The School of Engineering, founded in 1852, and the School of Art, founded in 1865, set the stage, and by the early decades of Yale's third century the University was educating its students in ways beyond conventional classroom experience. The School of Forestry, founded in 1901, addressed on the graduate level the seemingly antagonistic fields of environmental protection and scientific study of the uses of forest products. Engineering was taught in the new Mason Laboratory, and this branch of study enjoyed a burst of growth when the Sheffield Scientific School was finally absorbed by the University after World War II. Even the undergraduates got their hands dirty, and in the picture to the left we can see a typical print shop in the basement of a residential college, where students learned both the intellectual and material aspects of publishing through the creation of in-house printed matter. To this day presses, type, and inky aprons reside in many of the college basements.

48

49

48 *Printing on a clamshell letterpress in the print shop in the basement of Timothy Dwight College.* **49** *Mechanical engineering at the Dunham Laboratory. Two large American flags reflect the patriotic feelings afoot just before World War II.* **50** *Wood samples in the School of Forestry.*

When a group of well-off youngsters found themselves in such a magical world as old Yale, their energy could not be easily confined to the classroom. Some perpetrated typical college pranks, like this huge Y painted on East Rock. Others were drawn to a less public forum, the undergraduate societies that were scattered across the campus. By the 1940s only the senior societies and a few fraternities still existed, because the creation of the residential college system had so altered the living patterns on campus. Secret societies still exist at Yale, and their buildings sit like perfect jewel boxes, dotting the landscape. Members retain society privileges for life, and even though most students never cross their thresholds, these enigmatic buildings form an integral part of Yale's extended family.

51 East Rock, with painted graffiti. 52 Chipping off the paint with rock hammers. 53 A turn-of-the-century photograph of Scroll and Key. 54 Book and Snake today.

53

54

Here we see the evolution of undergraduate style, as evidenced by formal photographs of two Yale Promenade Committees. The 1931 Committee members seem old and serious; they look like our parents though probably no one in the picture had reached thirty years of age. The 1971 Committee members, on the other hand, simply look as though they are having a grand time as they make fun of some imagined—and rejected—formality. What they have in common, however, is the continuation of the tradition of holding the prom, ensuring that it is well run, and setting down a record of those who undertook the task of arranging the event. Whether grim and stiffly dressed or flip and irreverent in their poses, they betray the Yale undergraduate's long-standing habit of organization and competence.

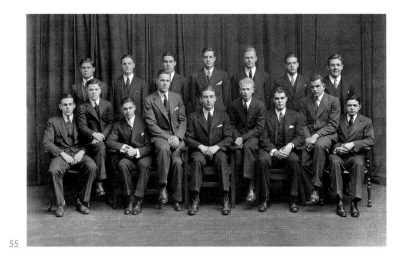

55

56

57

55 *The 1931 Junior Promenade Committee.* **56** *The 1971 Junior Promenade Committee.* **57** *A scene from the 1937 Junior Promenade.*

58

59

60

Student life at Yale is an ongoing cycle of days, comprising sleep, education, and various social events. The University itself experiences a greater cycle of years, with familiar months and their rituals recurring for decades and decades. One of the challenges Yale faces as a school is to live in this cyclical manner and yet still recognize that the students are experiencing a one-time educational process that has a beginning, a long and interesting middle, and a joyful and celebratory end. For every student the years at Yale are unique, and the faculty and administration must make this special time as good as can be, even though those who run the University have seen it all before. Four years of reluctant awakenings, bleary-eyed visits to Yale Station, and long hours of study finally come to an end with Commencement. What was yet another reprise for Yale has been a new and singular experience for the graduate; this is one of the major distinctions between the teachers and those who receive the lessons.

58 *A typical morning scene in the Yale residences.* **59** *Buying stamps at Yale Station.* **60** *A surveying class in the 1920s.* **61** *The annual ritual of planting the ivy, taking place in 1938.*

61

There are moments when a simple act carries tremendous meaning. In this photograph a student's pen hovers above the official document of enlistment. If he puts his signature on the sheet, the precious investment in his young life, from early childhood through the pleasure of his years at Yale, could all be swept away in the mindless happenstance of war. He might spiral down through the sky over the Pacific, meet his end in battle-scarred Europe, or simply spend four years being bored in some supply depot far from the enemy lines. Whatever the case, his signature on this day will mark an abrupt turn in the path of this young life.

62 *A Yale undergraduate signing enlistment papers for service in World War II. It is difficult to know whether this is a record of a real event or a publicity photograph posed to order. Whichever the case, the poignant act depicted here took place thousands of times on campuses across the country.* **63** *Members of the Naval Reserve Officers Training Corps marching on the Old Campus.* **64** *(overleaf) A mobile canteen donated to the British War Relief Society by the Yale Class of 1897.*

IV Life at Yale During World War II

The passage of time can be so deceptive. The construction of the residential colleges began less than a decade before World War II; change came at a tremendous pace during the first part of the century. Today young people have gotten the notion that they live in the most rapidly changing of times, but every recent generation has faced its own whirlwind of social and technological development. The canteen on the facing page is another example. This mobile food kitchen was donated to the British war effort in 1943 by the Yale College Class of 1897. Now mature and reaching the end of their working lives, these Yale grads were still actively involved in the bewildering events of midcentury.

Commencement Address, 1943

PRESIDENT CHARLES SEYMOUR

Since the founding of Yale in 1701 there have been eleven wars in which our American people have been involved. It is a fact which few of us have stopped to realize that in this period war has broken out on an average every twenty-two years. All but three of these wars were what we should today term global, involving all the great powers. Thus Yale is not facing a new experience, in that as an American institution we now find ourselves touched closely by military and naval events which may take place at a great physical distance from us. The so-called isolation which was supposed to provide us immunity from international warfare, its perils and its ravages, was indeed an illusion long before radio unified time and the airplane annihilated space.

A New Experience

It is true nonetheless that Yale, with the coming of this war, did face a new experience. For more than in any time in her history the University as an institution has gone to war. In our previous history our contribution to the war effort was largely indirect, through the patriotic service of our individual students and alumni. Of that service, and of the fact that Yale prepared them for it, we are very proud. The effect of the wars upon college life was varied. Those of the earlier part of the eighteenth century, the War of 1812, the Mexican, and Spanish wars hardly touched us. The War of the Revolution, on the other hand, endangered the very existence of the college; economic and financial conditions made normal life impossible; one class was sent to Wethersfield, another to Farmington, an expedition which nineteenth-century undergraduates would not have regarded as distasteful; the president-emeritus of the college, fighting single-handed on the road to Savin Rock, was captured by the invading British; the end of the Revolution found Yale approaching bankruptcy both in the financial and educational sense. The War between the States deprived us for decades of our important and esteemed undergraduate contingent from the South. The First World War swept the campus of our upper classes; had it been prolonged the entire undergraduate body might have been called away.

Yale has survived these wars and has increased her strength. We are now throwing that strength into the struggle for victory, a victory upon which depends the continued existence of all those things that make a university useful to the nation in times of peace. We have undertaken an active direct role in war service, through the contributions of our faculty and our laboratories, and as a training school for soldiers and sailors. It is with deep satisfaction that we can thus fulfill the terms of the resolution passed by the University Corporation within a week of the attack on Pearl Harbor which put at the disposition of the government for purposes of national defense not merely the physical facilities of Yale but also the capacities that peculiarly fit us to serve in the crisis. We are being used in the field where we are best trained: we are ordered to teach. This mission in relation to the war and the victory that is to follow Yale is proud to undertake.

FUSELAGE, B26, T.S. YALE

65

Yale adapted well, once again, to patriotic fervor, and the campus sprouted marching soldiers and accessories of war that seemed completely out of place among the elms and Gothic buildings. Men in uniform became commonplace, training sessions were held everywhere, and the academic and military ways of life cooperated to support the war effort.

65 *The remains of a B-26 bomber, resting in front of Dunham Laboratory.*
66 *On the left is Major Everett Parker Pope, Marine Corps winner of the Congressional Medal of Honor, being congratulated by Captain John J. Smith, who received the Navy Cross for his efforts on Guadalcanal.*
67 *Heading out to graduation ceremonies for the Yale Army Schools.*

66

67

68 *Military training exercises in the pool at the Payne Whitney Gymnasium, where the students are learning to swim underwater while fully clothed.* **69** *A group of Naval cadets from Yale on training duties outside Boston Harbor.*

The dictionary makes little distinction between training and education, but pictures of Yale during World War II are clearly about training for wartime, and not about the educational process as it is usually understood. The swimmers pictured at left, learning to escape underwater while fully clothed, are being forced into an alien and unlikely activity. If they should ever need this particular skill, their training will have acquainted them with previously unfamiliar territory. Education, on the other hand, is about the expansion of the mind through the opening of intellectual doors; education is about future growth, while training is about developing a specific skill. The University was the seat of both modes of learning during the war years. Graduation ceremonies, with academic robes and military uniforms side by side, provided strong evidence that Yale embraced two diverse developmental patterns for the students who attended while World War II was being waged.

68

69

V Postwar Yale

70 Planting seedlings at the School of Forestry during the 1940s.
71 Construction of Quonset huts near the Yale athletic fields. **72** (overleaf) Looking down on the row of new Quonset huts on Whitney Avenue, at the present location of parking lot 18.

Following the war thousands upon thousands of young men returned home and resumed the educations that they had left or began studies deferred by the emergency. Because World War II gave a tremendous boost to technological development, many of the returning GIs who came to Yale applied to study engineering. Yale had founded the School of Engineering as part of the Sheffield Scientific School in the nineteenth century, so the practical arts could be studied at Yale without disturbing the original ideal of higher education that had always been the mission of the College. In 1932 Engineering was made a separate school of the University, and engineering applicants swelled its rolls after the war. Today engineering at Yale is taught in the Department of Engineering and not in a separate professional school.

71

Once the fighting was over the University had to add Quonset huts to its architectural mélange, to house the huge influx of returning students. The buildings of Yale then ranged from Colonial through Victorian, mock medieval, modern, and finally the cylindrical rolled sheet metal of cheap temporary military housing. It is sad that no Yale professor of architectural history argued for the preservation of the Quonset huts, which might have become a distinctive piece of history for future generations.

In the account below, a graduate student's wife describes the trials, tribulations, and satisfactions of family life around the University.

The Distaff Side of Life at Yale

MARY E. COSTELLO

The presence of student wives at Yale has caused quite a change in the scene and atmosphere of the campus. The ubiquitous baby carriages block the entrance to Yale Station, impede pedestrian traffic on Wall Street, and trip the unwary who hurry out of Liggetts. White rows of diapers provide the landscaping for Sachemville (Quonset huts on Whitney Avenue) and Armoryville (ditto near the Bowl). The toddlers who enter George and Harry's crying, "Daddy, Daddy!" are no longer considered part of a premeditated design to embarrass a freshman on a heavy date. An even more outstanding change is noticed in the attitude of the wolf pack as compared to pre-war days. The slim and beautiful blonde standing on the corner of High and Elm does not now receive the low whistle or the whatcha-doing-tonight routine; her six-foot-three ex-Marine husband is too apt to have just stepped inside to collect the family mail.

The Married Set

Since there are now some 1,098 married veterans, the girls strolling through the college squares are more apt to be mothers and housewives than eager strays from Poughkeepsie. While the university social life used to center in the colleges, the married set moves in separate circles on the periphery. The campus cops have to check complaints of noise on Saturday nights in Yale houses on Lake Place, Wall Street, and in the once sedate homes on Temple and Hillhouse now converted into apartments.

The biggest topic of concern and general interest among the married element is the housing situation. It's always good for stirring up a group if the conversation lags. The Yale housing office has the thankless job of losing friends and alienating people by failing to provide suitable living quarters. Even though there are one hundred Quonset huts and a total of almost three hundred family accommodations provided by the University, some six hundred Yale couples have had to make arrangements in New Haven or neighboring towns.

The Quonset huts are each divided into two separate living units, with a kitchen–living room, two bedrooms, and a bath. Though they were regarded with a good deal of skepticism at first, the inhabitants of these compact little oddities have loyal praise for them as temporary homes. The houses which have been converted into family quarters are far more radical experiments in community living. Most couples are allotted two rooms and bath and kitchen privileges—meaning the privilege to share these utilities with one, two, or three other families. More fortunate ones have an extra room and/or a private bath, depending on the floor plan and plumbing facilities of the respective houses.

73

The social behavior of college undergraduates can be very strange. In the past they lived within a viciously stratified class system, and at Yale this was most evident during Tap Day, when seniors dashed across campus to pick the most desirable candidates for admittance into the senior societies or some of the University's many singing groups. It must be thrilling to be desired, to be the object of competition by upperclassmen, but some must always be left out, deemed unworthy or in some way unqualified. Such are the extremes of embrace or rejection by the intense community of one's own college.

74

73 Tap Day, when runners spiral off to pick the best candidates for their social groups. **74** Competition for the Tang Cup, in which teams from the residential colleges tried to out-drink one another under the pressures of the stopwatch. **75** A mock graduation held at the Yale Daily News. Pete Parke receives his honorary degree of Doctor of the Art of Mastering News (D.A.M.N.) in a tongue-in-cheek ceremony held in 1960. Parke covered Yale Commencements for years and regularly complained about never receiving a degree from the University. His colleagues at the news bureau obliged. **76** The Lampson Lions at a temporary resting place before ending up in their current home at the corner of Grove and Ashmun streets.

75

These red sandstone lions originally adorned Lampson Hall, which was the central building at the end of the old Berkeley Oval. When the residential colleges were built, the oval disappeared, and the lions were displaced from their exalted spot overseeing the courtyard. The Lampson Lions are almost comic in their demeanor and look as though they belong in some Alice in Wonderland tale, with tears rolling down their cold cheeks as they mourn their lost elevation. They were moved around for a while, and today they have come to rest at ground level, guarding the Grove Street entrance to the Yale power plant. The poor old dears are so sweet that even Yale's tough-minded facilities department can't bear to get rid of them.

76

77

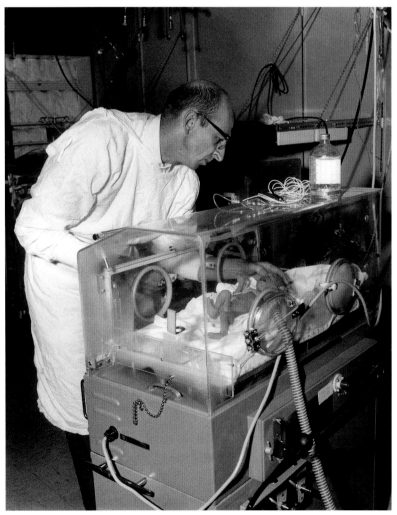

78

77 A view to downtown New Haven in 1954, south of Route 34, prior to the expansion of the Yale School of Medicine. *78* Tending a baby born prematurely at the Yale–New Haven Hospital. *79* A drawing of a nerve fiber, by the neuron researcher Santiago Ramón y Cajal. *80* A photomicrograph of a nerve fiber, produced in the laboratory of Professor Stephen G. Waxman.

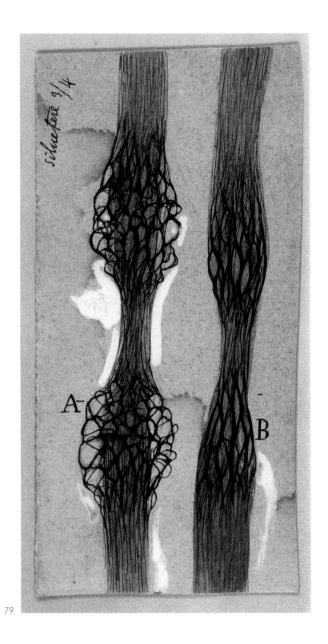

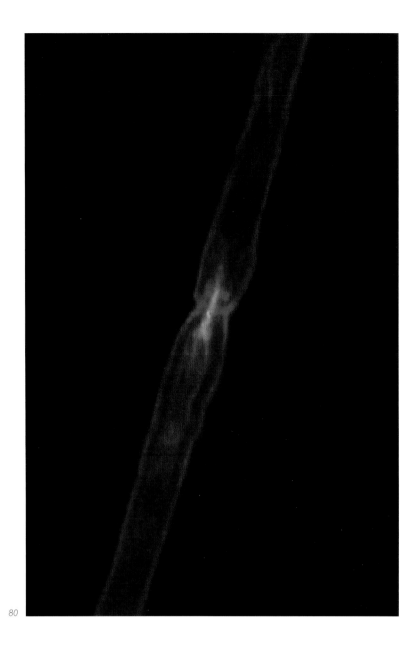

79

80

Throughout its long history, medicine has possessed two radically different natures. One is visible in the lower picture on the facing page, where a doctor reaches into an incubator at Yale–New Haven Hospital. His hand curves around the baby's head in a sensitive and telling touch, and physical contact with his tiny patient gives the doctor a direct diagnostic message. Medicine's other side is clearly revealed in the two pictures at the top of this page. They are visual records of nerve structure, and they demonstrate the continual scientific probing that made possible the remarkable strides in medicine of the twentieth century. Whether the doctor lived centuries ago or works today in a modern hospital, the task is much the same: to be sensitive to the organism as a whole, and to develop methods for the simultaneous maintainence and repair of the biological machine.

The drawing on the left, beautiful in its design and hand rendition, shows visual evidence of an artist-researcher's mind struggling to make sense out of a microscopic view. The photograph on the right, made at a vastly greater enlargement, shows direct evidence of a structure that exists by the hundreds of millions in each of us. The tiny nerve junction is a hitherto invisible building block of the animal world that has been revealed through our obsessive efforts to understand the miracle of life. The formidable task of Yale's School of Medicine is to balance the importance of this microscopic fact with the doctor's age-old touch.

The primary missions of Yale are research and education. We give so much attention to Yale's buildings, history, alumni, athletics, and faculty that we can easily forget that teaching is a large part of what we are meant to be doing, and all facets of the University should, in some way, serve this fundamental task. One of the hallmarks of a Yale education is that professors at the very top of their fields spend the time and energy necessary to teach at the undergraduate level. The finest and most highly respected minds bend themselves to the most fundamental kind of higher education.

This teacher is William Kurtz Wimsatt Jr., Sterling Professor of English. He taught at Yale from 1939 to 1975, and he was the author of numerous books of English literary criticism. Wimsatt's *Verbal Icon* was in the forefront of the New Criticism, and it contains some of the densest thinking imaginable about theories of language. He also wrote the definitive work on the portraits of Alexander Pope (one of which hangs over his shoulder). In his spare time, he was a chess master who wrote on the structures and pleasures of chess problems.

Here he is, hands spread in a gesture of emphasis, introducing intellectual problems to young students, some of whom may have only an inkling of the stature of the man with whom they are exchanging ideas.

81 William K. Wimsatt holding a class in his office at Silliman College. **82** Lawrence Paros, director of the Yale Summer High School, contemplating a student question. **83** Peter Kindlmann adjusting a vernier chronotron.

Yale's summer high school drew approximately 150 students from New Haven and surrounding towns. They took up residence in the buildings of the Yale Divinity School, where they received an educational boost that helped many move on to a college career. The pensive teacher in this picture is Lawrence Paros, director of the Yale Summer High School, who taught for many years in the New Haven school system.

This photograph shows Peter Kindlmann, a graduate student in the department of Engineering and Applied Science, working on a vernier chronotron, which was used in research on early gas lasers. Peter graduated and embarked upon a career in electrical engineering, but he also taught at Yale and achieved adjunct status in 1979. Many of the University's most valued faculty members are adjunct. The position requires only part-time teaching, relatively free of administrative work, so adjuncts can simultaneously pursue careers in their fields. Peter did so for years, but now, thirty-six years after this picture was taken, he has become a full-time professor, acting as the director of undergraduate studies in electrical engineering.

84

85

84 Lars Onsager, winner of the 1968 Nobel Prize in chemistry for his theory of irreversible chemical processes, playing his home-made bass fiddle with some cronies from the chemistry department. **85** Barbara Bonnardi, who worked in the Yale Admissions Office for forty-eight years. **86** The dedication of the Wright nuclear accelerator, in 1964. At left is Allan Bromley, who, after a career at Yale and then service in Washington, D.C., with the National Science Foundation, returned to Yale in 1993 and a year later became the dean of engineering. Second from left is Glenn T. Seaborg, then commissioner of atomic energy, and third from right is Kingman Brewster, then President of Yale.

VI Athletics at Yale

Physical education has a long tradition at institutions of higher education. In the following excerpts from addresses by Martin Griffin, dean of undergraduate studies, and President A. Bartlett Giamatti, physical education is placed in the purest of contexts, through parallels with the education of the mind. This ideal has been violated by the practice of athletic recruitment at many universities, and Yale's reluctance to aggressively recruit has resulted in a steadily shrinking pool of comparable institutions against which our students can effectively compete.

Athletics as Part of a Liberal Education
December 1982
MARTIN GRIFFIN

It has long been recognized at liberal arts colleges that while there is a large area of intersection between what is "academic" and what is "educational," the word "educational" is the larger and more encompassing term and includes matters "academic." Ever since the nineteenth century, certain extracurricular activities have played an important role in providing a liberal education at Yale by supplementing the formal curriculum with experiences that assist in the development of the student as a whole person, help in the formation of his character, and aid in determining some of the basic features of his personality.

In fact, it might be said that many of the lessons learned in the extracurriculum may be crucial to the long-range effectiveness of the curriculum itself in a person's life. This is because a liberal education is not defined only and solely by its academic component. Part of a liberal education is constituted by those experiences or extracurricular activities that enable an individual to give fuller force and potency to his academic training. I have said elsewhere in this letter that "a liberal education aims at making a person a better human being. 'Its focus on the intellectual and moral development of the individual' is intended to make the individual a finer and more effective person, with all that such a goal implies." Thus the lessons of those extracurricular experiences and activities that aid in the formation of a person's character and personality may be described as the enabling features of a liberal education, helping to give it efficacy in the daily transactions of an individual's affairs, both large and small, throughout his lifetime.

Athletics stands high among the extra-academic activities that constitute such a part of a liberal education. The lessons it teaches are many, and they are enduring. Among them are learning how to play fairly, to discipline oneself, to make decisions quickly, to maintain dignity under adversity, to respect both teammates and adversaries, to strive for excellence for the sake of excellence, to win gracefully and to lose gracefully, to play with honor and honesty within the constraints of rules, to make sacrifices, to persevere when all seems lost, and to develop a sense of obligation and responsibility for others in one's group. These lessons make athletics an academy of the emotions and a school for character, and for the athlete it represents an intrinsic and invaluable part of the non-academic aspects of his liberal education.

If all this be true, then coaches are teachers in the fullest sense of the word, and are essential participants in the achievement of Yale College's educational goals. They are the chief agents by which the University makes athletics part of a liberal education. As teachers, counselors, and mentors of their students, they encourage athletes to learn and practice and teach each other those lessons that make athletics part of a liberal education. They help to make each athlete the best athlete that he can be, not just to win, but also to encourage excellence for the sake of excellence. They help their students to see that beyond victory or defeat there are lessons to be learned in athletics that will endure throughout a lifetime.

Association of Yale Alumni Assembly XVI

April 10, 1980

A. BARTLETT GIAMATTI

An ideal of education, and of the proper place of athletics within it, should be with us to this day, in this place, and must shape our thinking. Such a liberal education, properly understood, supports athletics as an essential part of the educational process. It is equally consistent with this view, however, that athletics not outstrip that larger process, or deviate from it. Such an ideal means that we no more encourage a professionalism of spirit in athletics in our undergraduates than we encourage a professional view of the purpose of an undergraduate education. It means we believe in an education that is a process of exploration and fulfillment, not a process of pursuing a career.

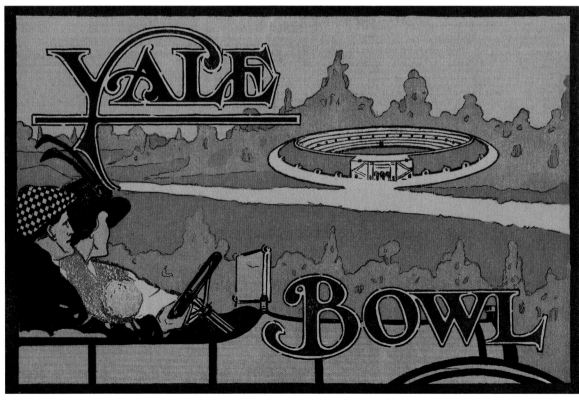

88 *The Yale Bowl, under construction. The circular outer retaining wall holds in place the earth removed from the center excavation of the playing field. The Bowl thus follows a pattern of construction developed in the amphitheaters of the ancient world.* **89** *The cover of the program for the Bowl's dedication ceremony, November 21, 1914.* **90** *An early color photograph of the Bowl, taken on opening day, before the crowds were admitted.*

88

90

One of the oldest established practices at Yale is to name a facility for its primary donor, or in honor of some influential figure. Many of the venues visible in an aerial view of the athletic complex bear a prominent name. The varsity football arena is an exception, called simply the Yale Bowl, but below it on the left is the Coxe Cage, on the right is the Walter Camp Memorial Gateway, and in between is the Joel F. Smilow Field House. Nestled between the Cage and the Gateway are the Culman indoor and outdoor tennis courts. Across Derby Avenue we see Yale Field on the right, and at left is the DeWitt Cuyler Athletic Field. Inside this field's track is a football field named in honor of Clinton E. Frank. In many cases the funding to Yale comes from an alumnus who honors the part of Yale life that meant the most to him during undergraduate years. In others donations are made so that the Yale graduate can give something back in a manner that best fits the University's current needs. Yale benefits from the connection, the donor's name becomes part of the Yale lexicon, and for years afterward the names are used with warm familiarity during talk about the good old days at school.

91 A New Haven trolley car on its way to the Yale Bowl. 92 An aerial view of the athletic complex taken in the mid-seventies.

93

This is certainly a picture of some famous people. The top-heavy gent on the left is Babe Ruth, the greatest slugger of all time. He has come to West Haven on June 5, 1948, just a few months before his death, to give the original manuscript of his memoirs to the Yale University Library, accepted by the captain of the varsity baseball team. That fellow, the tall and slender one in the pinstriped uniform, is George Bush. This photo has been published on a number of occasions, a popular bit of Americana that brings together a mythic sports hero and a future president. But the picture usually is printed with only these two men showing, cropping out the short man to the right. This version adds another famous figure at Yale. His name is Robert Kiphuth, who coached the Yale

swimmers through their glory years from the twenties through the fifties, then became Yale's athletic director until 1959. Kiphuth was the embodiment of sports at Yale, and he probably arranged the meeting recorded in this photograph.

*93 The Babe at Yale Field in 1948. **94** A cartoon by Garry Trudeau on the subject of the 1968 Yale-Harvard game. **95** A play from that game, with Brian Dowling (10) carrying the ball and Calvin Hill (30) waiting for a pass.*

74

94

95

It is impossible to discuss football at Yale without acknowledging the existence of the 1968 Yale-Harvard game. Yale led by sixteen points with forty-two seconds to go, and, as with the famous Dewey "defeat" of Truman, the press folks were already filing their stories of Yale's great victory. Harvard scored a touchdown, added a two-point conversion, and cut the lead to eight. On the ensuing kickoff, Harvard recovered an onside dribbler, and with three seconds left, the Crimson scored another touchdown. A pass into the end zone for another two-point conversion tied the game. The Elis have been blushing ever since with embarrassment over the 29–29 "loss."

96

What is wrong with this picture? The Payne Whitney Gymnasium stands up so clearly, with its full facade visible, that it almost looks like an architect's model, made to sell the Corporation on the idea of a cathedral for sport. The trouble with this interpretation of the picture is that those cars in the foreground, shrieking of the fifties with their perfectly detailed fins, chrome, and bulbous fenders, are not models but the real things.

What is odd about the photograph is that Morse and Ezra Stiles colleges are absent, not yet constructed. In their absence the gym fronts on a large temporary parking lot that has replaced three New Haven high schools, Hillhouse, Boardman, and Wilbur Cross. The last of the schools came down in 1958, and the new residential colleges, funded by Paul Mellon, were built in 1962. Payne Whitney had only three years during which its immense form could be viewed with ease from behind the Hall of Graduate Studies.

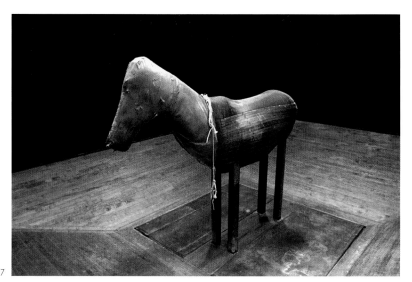

97

98

99

96 The Payne Whitney Gymnasium, probably photographed from the roof of Sterling Memorial Library. **97** The practice polo pony on the gymnasium's fourth floor. **98** Exhibition Pool during a meet in the 1950s. **99** Family Day, when local youths were invited to the Payne Whitney pool.

100

101

100 *The Yale Bowl, full to the brim, on the occasion of the one hundredth Yale-Harvard game, 1983.* **101** *A. Bartlett Giamatti conducting the band at the one hundredth game.* **102** *A young faculty couple with their family at the Yale Bowl during the 1980s.* **103** *Carm Cozza and Joe Restic at Restic's final game, at Yale in 1993.*

Carm Cozza was the head football coach at Yale for thirty-two years, and his counterpart at Harvard, Joe Restic, led the Crimson team for twenty-two years. When the time came for their respective retirements, each coach chose to step down after a Yale-Harvard game that was played at his rival's home stadium. This picture shows the two coaches after the 1993 game at the Yale Bowl, Restic's final one. Cozza retired three years later, after the Harvard-Yale game at Harvard Stadium. Each coach chose to go out in the quietest manner possible, diverting attention from himself through this clever bit of career planning. Doubtless they plotted the whole thing together.

102

103

104

104 *The varsity women's basketball team playing its final game to win the Ivy League title in 1989.* 105 *Celebrating after the game.* 106 *Junior varsity crew practice in the tanks in the basement of the Payne Whitney Gymnasium.* 107 *A race on the Housatonic River on Derby Day, 1947.*

105

Rowing has been taken seriously at Yale for more than a century and a half. The old boathouse, nestled beneath the Q Bridge, has long since been sold by the University and now faces demolition. Daily practice takes place on the Housatonic River in Derby or in the tanks in the basement of the Payne Whitney Gymnasium. Any picture of a shell shows the row of students who make up the boat's team, and long hours sweating and tuning up as a unit connect the crew in deep and unforgettable ways. When students leave Yale, their long-term friends come as often from their athletic experience as from their colleges or classrooms.

106

107

VII The Turmoil of the Sixties and Seventies

Yale went into the sixties with business as usual. The University expanded, through construction of Morse and Ezra Stiles colleges and the growth of Science Hill; plans for two more residential colleges never got off the drawing board. As Yale grew and grew, so too did the task of administering such a large and complex entity. The social and technological revolutions of the late sixties and seventies were brewing. An all-male undergraduate population gave way to coeducation in the early seventies. Vacuum tubes gave way to transistors, ushering in the computer age. And the troublesome war in Vietnam transformed a new generation into the parents of our modern society.

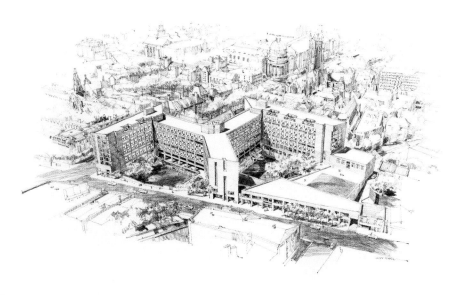

108

109

110

What a remarkable photograph this is. Carl Roessler, Yale's director of computation, sits at his desk surrounded by the old and new tools of the information age. His eyes rest on a printed page, the oldest and by far the most powerful tool yet invented for recording and disseminating the workings of the human mind. To the right of the book is a typewriter converted into a Teletype machine, a clacking electro-mechanical device at the forefront of moving verbal information through the new ether of electronic space. Next to the typewriter is a telephone, but an unusual one, sitting in an unfamiliar holder. This, believe it or not, is an early modem, years before the Internet made information readily available over phone lines. Next to the modem is a primitive computer. What Hollywood screenwriter would have had the ironic inspiration to name it SEER, and how prophetic the name. The black screen holds plain letters, hopelessly crude compared to today's typographic miracles that come from the power of the Postscript language. This odd-looking machine was to grow sleek

and become embedded in our society in ways unthinkable in the 1960s, and a similar-sized machine, on any faculty desk today, has computing power that easily exceeds that of Yale, New Haven, and probably all of Connecticut at the time this photograph was taken.

108 A drawing for a residential college that was never constructed. 109 Administrative filing before the advent of the digital office. 110 Carl Roessler with the data tools used early in the transition from analog to digital.

111

In the mid-1950s two student-driven riots took place near the corner of Elm and High streets. The bigger of the two was the snowball riot, precipitated by a heavy, wet spring snow, the sort that was perfect for making snowballs. Freshmen, upperclassmen, and participants in the Saint Patrick's Day parade were all swept up in a grand melee, and by the time it was all over there had been a full-fledged confrontation, with police, motorcycles, and even A. Whitney Griswold, who tried to calm things down. Rooms in Saybrook and Calhoun were invaded by police, and vain attempts were made to haul the Yalies down to the station, but when it was all over the main impact was amazement that such an irrational event had ever taken place. Little did the participants imagine the significance that confrontations between students and the law were to assume in the coming decades.

112

*111–112 Two scenes from the St. Patrick's Day snowball riot. **113** President Griswold surveying the damage after the confrontation between police and Yale students had ended in the snowball riot. **114** A news shot of the Humpty Dumpty man and his cart in the midst of the ice cream riot.*

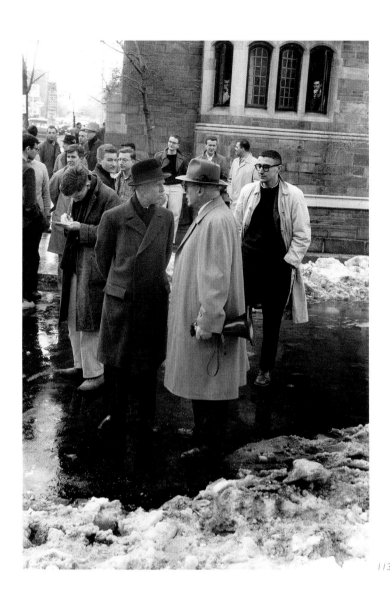

113

114

NXP403-5/13-NEW HAVEN,CONN.:Cheering Yale students mill around an ice-cream vendor 5/13 during 1,500-student demonstration against chasing of vendors from the campus gate by police.The riot was staged near historic Central Green,scene of many riots by students in past years.Four students and two ice-cream salesmen were arrested.UNITED PRESS TELEPHOTO ld

CLASS IV. U. S. ARMY CIVIL AFFAIRS TRAINING SCHOOL, FAR EASTERN AFFAIRS, YALE UNIVERSITY, AUGUST 1945

Jay Storm
New Haven, Conn.

Top Row (Left to right): Lt. A. Hurwitt, C. E.; Lt. C. van Zwoll, Sig. C.; Maj. E. V. Hays, C. M. P.; Lt. R. C. Ward, Q. M. C.; Lt. R. J. Venrose, M. A. C.; Maj. G. W. Myers, M. A. C.; Capt. C. J. Young, A. C.; Lt. H. L. Silverman, A. U. S.; Lt. A. J. Theodore, Q. M. C.

Third Row (Left to right): Capt. H. L. Weary, A. C.; Capt. C. E. Tuttle, C. W. S.; Lt. R. L. Perlman, C. W. S.; Capt. R. F. Pugh, Royal Arty.; Maj. E. M. Galloway, Royal Arty.; Capt. D. H. Wells, Q. M. C.; Lt. L. G. Winzenburg, C. A. C.; Capt. J. G. Mac Innis, Royal Arty.; Lt. P. S. Anderson, C. M. P.; Lt. V. A. Johnson, M. A. C.; Lt. H. J. Knapp, Sig. C.; Lt. F. B. Tracy, A. U. S.; Capt. T. H. Stratton, C. M. P.; Lt. H. Z. Leveille, C. M. P.

Second Row (Left to right): Capt. G. T. Cooper, C. E.; Lt. R. L. Park, C. M. P.; Capt. T. A. Mullaney, A. C.; Capt. T. G. Beebe, F. A.; Lt. C. F. Moses, F. A.; Lt. R. E. Mac Phaul, C. E.; Lt. J. J. Silva, C. E.; Capt. A. F. Andrade, A. C.; Capt. R. Murdock, Canadian Army Inf.; Capt. Andrew W. S. In, Inf.; Maj. G. R. Dougherty, A. C.; Lt. P. E. Du Parc, Jr., C. E.; Capt. W. B. Hall, C. E.; Lt. J. F. Griffin, Cav.; Lt. W. M. Cranstoun, Sig. C.; Capt. P. L. Foster, A. C.; Capt. J. W. King, C. E.

Bottom Row (Left to right): Maj. A. B. Chun, Inf.; Maj. F. K. Dillon, A. C.; Maj. L. D. Gritman, T. C.; Maj. H. W. Pardee, A. C.; Maj. C. W. Barton, Sn.C.;Maj. R. J. Aldrich, Q. M. C.; Maj. D. W. Bennett, A. C.; Maj. E. L. Turbyfill, Inf.; Maj. M. P. Brown, C. E.; Lt. Col. W. P. Bogie, Inf.; Lt. Col. H. O. Benton, A. C.; Lt. Col. L. B. Thompson, Inf.; Lt. Col. W. H. Gordon, Inf.; Lt. Col. G. H. Harding, Engrs.; Maj. D. D. Jeter, Cav.; Lt. Col. J. E. Wilson, A. C.; Pres.

If we build the physical structures of the University well, then they can adapt themselves to uses unimagined by their builders. A case in point is Woolsey Hall, where, in the late sixties, Jimi Hendrix held one of his greatest concerts, blowing the building's main fuse with the first chord of his guitar. The Cenotaph outside Commons is another example. If the builders had any idea of the students' potential relation to this monument, the picture on the left would probably have been what they had in mind: a graduating class of cadets shortly before the end of World War II. A few years later this noble memorial was the backdrop for scenes like the one on the right, when the protests of the sixties and seventies reached full swing. The ordered ranks of obedient youth have transformed into unruly and outspoken zealots who fit no comfortable pigeonhole in the minds of their elders. Each of the groups pictured here represents an extreme of behavior, and the columns and carvings of Yale remain steady through the violent swings of social change.

116

115 A graduation picture of the 1945 U.S. Army Civil Affairs Training School. **116** Students for a Democratic Society holding a demonstration in front of the Cenotaph outside Commons in 1971.

The burdens of any presidency vary according to prevailing conditions. When times are good—that is to say, calm, productive, and economically and educationally healthy—then the leader of a university faces the task of steering the organization so that it will take the best course through the anticipated future. A large institution such as Yale changes direction very slowly, and, once set on a path, stubbornly resists corrective turns. This means that the President's performance is revealed only in years to come, long after anything can be done to correct errors of judgment. When times are bad—when turmoil threatens the safety of the University—then the President has the excruciating duty to be decisive on issues that divide the community. No matter what he or she does, someone will feel betrayed and disappointed, and often, when the decision is the wisest one, many will feel let down by their leader.

In the violent times of the late sixties and early seventies, Kingman Brewster led Yale. This elegant patrician, seen here with his family at their summer retreat on Martha's Vineyard, had to balance Yale's precious and out-of-date sense of itself with the long-overdue revolution in human rights that was remaking our country. He faced hard choices and handled

Yale's entry into the new times far more effectively than any comparable university leader. The radicals and the conservatives all thought that he should have done things somewhat differently, but Yale lived through these times and came out a far better institution than it had been before. Brewster stood his ground and voiced his beliefs with constraint and grace. Since his Presidency tens of thousands of men and women have graduated from Yale, and they have had the benefit of studying at a great school whose modern image was in large part shaped by this man.

117 *Kingman and Mary Louise Brewster with their family on Martha's Vineyard in the late sixties. From left to right: Kingman 3d, Constance, Kingman Jr., Alden, Riley, Mary Louise, Deborah, and, in the foreground, Gulliver, the family's black Labrador retriever.*

The letter excerpted below was written by Kingman Brewster to a concerned alumnus Mr. John C. Morrison of White Plains, New York. It perfectly expressed how the President grappled with the conflict between the need to be personally honest and the responsibility to represent the University in any public utterance he might make. Brewster's statements in this letter illustrate his beliefs at the height of the controversies over racial and social equality stirred by the the Black Panther trials in New Haven.

Kingman Brewster to John C. Morrison
May 1970

I appreciate your worry about statements on controversial issues, especially when they do not relate to Yale or even to education. Even when I disclaim any institutional spokesmanship and insist that my views are purely personal, I do realize that my office may in some eyes implicate Yale in anything I say or in any political position I may take.

This bothers me because I do feel very strongly that institutional neutrality on political matters is very important. It is essential for the preservation of academic freedom. If Yale had a "party line," then faculty and students might be inhibited in their own freedom of expression. Institutional neutrality is also essential if we are to continue to deserve the confidence of the public. Our privileges and immunities would eventually be withdrawn if it were felt that they were being used to push a particular dogma rather than for unfettered education and scholarship.

At the same time personal neutrality—an unwillingness to stand up and be counted on issues which grip the university community—seems to me unacceptable. Both educational and moral leadership require that a man say where he stands.

The young are quick to detect hypocrisy. They do not admire timidity. If a college president were not willing to avow his own convictions on controversial matters, he would properly be suspected of being a bland, faceless person. It would be quickly assumed that his dominant motive was to avoid antagonizing any source of support.

The Fellows of the Yale Corporation and I are convinced that this will be a better university if its President feels not only a freedom but an obligation to speak his mind about public matters of vital concern to all members of the university community, provided he makes it clear that he is speaking for himself, not for Yale.

On balance it is also our conviction that even institutional neutrality will be better protected if personal opinions may be outspoken. The effort to capture or pressure the university itself for a political purpose is easier to fend off if it can be demonstrated that institutional neutrality is a matter of policy and principle, not just a cloak to conceal personal timidity.

We are aware that this policy is neither riskless nor costless. Nothing in this office makes the President less fallible than his fellow citizens. The demands of today's instant, live journalism are full of booby traps. Even if errors and misunderstandings could be entirely avoided, our times are so ripped by controversy and divisions among us that there is almost no position which will not arouse bitter hostility in some quarters.

Thank you for your letter and the understandable concern which prompted it.

118

118 William Sloane Coffin, Chaplain to the University between 1958 and 1975, preaching from his pulpit. **119–120** Demonstrations on the streets of New Haven during the time of the Black Panther trials.

119

120

121

122

For most of its life Yale was an institution that had a single homogeneous population; it was male, affluent, and, as often as not, WASP. When society started to change in the sixties, the old University found its population evolving. There had always been a small Jewish contingent at Yale, and this percentage increased. People of color were welcomed, and—in an even greater break with tradition—women arrived on the scene. The University began to accommodate diverse points of view, which may or may not be accompanied by diversity of skin color, ethnicity, or sexual orientation. By the mid-seventies, the earlier conservative nature of the population had been transformed. At graduation a trim and uniformed young military man might find himself seated near a long-haired radical convinced that a bit of anarchy would make the world a better place. The comfort of cultural isolation had finally been swept away, and the richness of Yale's internal life has grown steadily since.

123

124

125 Three members of the Class of 1971 having lunch in the dining hall of Berkeley College. Women first came to Yale College in 1969, but many of them transferred to the University in their sophomore or junior years, and so graduated sooner than those who enrolled in the Class of 1973. This picture is from the archives of the Yale University News Bureau, and its obvious intention was to show the world at large that the unthinkable was taking place at Yale. Not only were women there, but they fit perfectly into the old school. **126** The first varsity women's athletic team at Yale.

127

The spirit of the sixties and seventies has lived on in student life, and protests have become a permanent part of the educational scene. This is a healthy sign, because a mature faculty serves a youthful population that often has insights that are unavailable to older generations. We must balance our desire for order with the chaos inherent in change and acknowledge that uprising students often have a pretty good point to make. These ramshackle huts, erected outside the Beinecke Library in 1988, were raised in protest of apartheid in South Africa. The shacks infuriated those who wanted the isolated world of Yale to be free of such disorder, but the protesters were more concerned that human beings be free of oppression. The shacks were set on fire one night, and the remains were unceremoniously carted away shortly thereafter.

128

129

In the midst of the demonstrations and social upheaval of the sixties and seventies, Yale's development on more traditional lines continued unabated. The earlier determination to make Yale a great university, with strengths in science as well as the humanities, demanded heavy investments on the north end of campus, and one of the primary donors there was C. Mahlon Kline. Kline's donations to the University created the Kline Chemistry Laboratory, the Kline Geology Laboratory, and the Kline Biology Tower. These buildings, constructed in the early sixties, transformed science at Yale. Student activism reshaped the culture at Yale, and the flowering of science created the University's worldwide reputation as a research institution. The rich achievements of the past quarter-century at Yale have built on these two legacies of the postwar era.

*127 The shacks of Winnie Mandela City, set up outside the Beinecke Library in 1988. **128** Taking down the charred remains of the shacks after their late-night burning. **129** C. Mahlon Kline, with Mary Louise and Kingman Brewster, on the occasion of the dedication of the Kline Biology Tower.*

University Arts

JULES D. PROWN

Paul Mellon Professor Emeritus History of Art

The arts flourish at Yale. They permeate the institution, enhancing not only scholarship and creativity but the very quality of life at the University and in New Haven. In music, drama, architecture, and the visual arts, a vibrant symbiotic relationship exists between the professional schools and the academic departments and programs that offer graduate and undergraduate education in both the history and practice of the arts. Great collections of art, books, manuscripts, and other research materials undergird the primary educational mission. The Yale University Art Gallery and the Yale Center for British Art are prominent, reinforced by extraordinary art resources in the Sterling, Beinecke, and Lewis Walpole libraries, the Peabody Museum, the Musical Instruments Collection, and other collections throughout the University. Creativity in drama, music, and art marks undergraduate life in University-wide organizations (the Dramat, Symphony, Glee Club, Marching Band), in specialized singing and performance groups (the Whiffenpoofs, the Russian Chorus, the Children's Theatre), and in frequent performances and exhibitions in the colleges and cultural houses. Art is everywhere.

Yale was home to the first university art gallery in the United States in 1832 and to the first university art school in 1869. But the exuberant flowering of the arts that now characterizes Yale occurred in the second half of the twentieth century. For me, personally, the major revolution occurred in the Art Gallery, precipitated by the arrival of a new director, Andrew Ritchie. When he came to Yale in 1956, Ritchie had already recorded a distinguished museum career as director of the Albright-Knox Museum in Buffalo and, more recently, curator of painting and sculpture at the Museum of Modern Art in New York. Ritchie immediately set about professionalizing the Gallery, which had languished for a few years following completion of the new Louis Kahn building. He began by changing all of the locks, alienating the senior history of art faculty, who had enjoyed unhampered access. Then, to the horror of architectural purists (including me), he transformed the interior of the Kahn building into a Museum of Modern Art clone. He covered the cinder block walls and many windows with white drywall panels, which, along with white pogo panel space dividers, provided more surface area for displaying works of art. The group of major alumni collectors who had enticed Ritchie to come to Yale approved of the interior transformation. Ritchie capitalized on their support by mounting a major exhibition of Art from Alumni Collections (1958), and he encouraged much more active alumni advisory involvement in the life of the Gallery. This in turn opened the door to a flow of alumni gifts and bequests of artworks, as well as enhanced financial support.

When I was offered a teaching job as an instructor at Yale in 1961, I telephoned Ritchie to get assurances about the accessibility of the unparalleled American collections in the Gallery for my teaching. "Can't talk now," he said. "The gym is flooding and I have to check on our Currier and Ives prints over there. I'll call you back." He did, and gave me warm encouragement. The next year I was named curator designate of American Art at the Gallery and was invited to work as Ritchie's assistant on a Ford Foundation project that involved visiting art and art history departments and university art museums around the country, leading to a publication on *Higher Education in the Visual Arts in the United States* (1966).

Andrew Ritchie's dominant passion was acquiring works of art for the Gallery. He was a bluff, hearty Scot with a flushed face, fringes of white hair, and large black-rimmed eyeglasses. Extremely social and convivial, devoted to parties and martinis, he was also invariably, often bluntly, honest. Once a potential donor offered to make a substantial financial gift to the Gallery along with a painting if Andrew would accept it as a Goya. Andrew said he would be happy to take the money, but as for the picture, "That's no Goya!" Later the man launched into some unfavorable remarks about Jews. Andrew cut him off, saying "I'm a committed philosemite, and have no use for this."

Even better than acquisition by gift or bequest for Andrew was buying a great work of art himself from the limited acquisition funds at his disposal. Although his greatest passion was for modern, especially contemporary, art, he had a superb eye and his taste was catholic. In 1962 he seized an opportunity to buy a version of Hiram Powers's great sculpture *The Greek Slave,* originally commissioned in Italy circa 1847 by Prince Demidoff. Beautifully carved and in exceptionally fine condition, the sculpture was soon displayed in a place of honor among the American collections in the Long Gallery on the third floor. Several months later, the Greek slave's right breast began gradually to turn black. This aroused considerable concern. Was there some flaw in the material—what conservators call "inherent vice"—coming to the surface, or was this evidence of an earlier restoration? Amid a flurry of consternation, the building superintendent, Carl Greene, had an idea.

When the night watchman came on duty, Greene accompanied him on his rounds. They proceeded through the Gallery, the watchman punching in with his time clock at the appropriate stations. Eventually they came to the Long Gallery. The watchman punched in at the entrance and continued through the room. As they passed *The Greek Slave,* Greene stopped and asked the watchman whether he did anything else in that room. After repeated denials, the watchman finally admitted that as he passed the sculpture on each round, he would give the slave's breast a little tweak—with a hand stained by the imitation black leather covering of his time clock. Repeated fondling had caused the marble breast to blacken. No "inherent vice" here, just a venial human weakness—would that all moral lapses washed off so easily.

Andrew Ritchie's enlightened, energetic leadership of the Art Gallery, and his efforts to enhance the collections and build alumni support, were carried forward, with greater emphasis on public programs, by his successors, notably Alan Shestack and Mimi Neill. Today the Gallery, under the energetic leadership of Jock Reynolds, continues to flourish, thanks in no small measure to the enhanced alumni involvement that Andrew Ritchie generated. That process has been and is being carried forward by devoted alumni whose generous support in the form of new and rehabilitated buildings, gifts of great works of art, and financial provision for staff and programs ensures that the arts at Yale will continue to thrive and serve the University at the highest possible level in the twenty-first century.

There has been talk for many years about Yale's role as the great cultural asset of New Haven, but this notion slights one of the great New England cities. New Haven has houses of all periods, from Colonial to modern, it has a Green unrivaled in New England, and it boasts the Grove Street Cemetery, which is one of the most beautiful resting places in the United States. The cemetery holds many of the town's early tombstones that were removed from their original site on the Green. The great Egyptian-style gateway seen in this photograph bears the motto "The Dead shall be raised." Locals like to point out that they already have been.

130 A view through the massive red sandstone gate of the Grove Street Cemetery, showing the small Victorian gatehouse within. 131 Old and new art on Hewitt Quadrangle.

This scene on Hewitt Quadrangle shows the base of the Led-yard Flagstaff and an Alexander Calder sculpture, both seen against the north side of Woodbridge Hall. The flagpole grows out of an ornate cast bronze base, with wreaths, grinning faces, flutes, and geometrical designs covering its every square inch. The Calder is plain by comparison, and the contrast between these two pieces brings home the changes that have occurred in art during the past century. The flagpole exemplifies nineteenth-century art with its grand but degenerate tradition of ponderous decoration. The modernity of the Calder speaks of a rebellion against this earlier taste. The red mobile's design is simple and engaging, and it sounds a note of lightheartedness among the classical patterns of Yale's bicentennial buildings. The Calder recently received a fresh coat of paint; color is an integral part of today's art, in the same way that polychrome sculpture was common in ancient Greece, and the red coating of the sculpture's base had already faded to a muted shade. The bronze flagpole support can go untouched for decades and still look right. The modern sculpture is delicate and fugitive; like many of the works of this century, it is a transitory and fragile thing.

132 The three panels of the large Tiffany window in Linsly-Chittenden, restored in 1998 during the building's modernization. 133 Room 102 before its renovation. 134 A portrait of Thorstein Veblen, painted by Edwin B. Child, hanging in room 211 of the Hall of Graduate Studies.

The halls of Yale are full of painted portraits of notable figures from the University's past. These are almost all men, and most of the paintings are, to be quite frank, unremarkable. Notable exceptions turn up; for example, there are a large number of Dean Keller portraits at Yale. He was a fine painter who carefully arrayed the attributes of the various professors in the backgrounds of the pictures, and his portraits usually convince us of their truth by the strength of the likenesses. A marvelous portrait of Thorstein Veblen painted by Edwin B. Child in 1934 hangs on the second floor of the Hall of Graduate Studies. Today the afternoon sun pours into this meeting room and gives a sparkle to the old economist's jaunty pose, as he lifts his cigarette and looks out at the modern people gathered in his oak-lined haunt.

135

136

137

Not all the art at Yale hangs in galleries or resides in warm wood-paneled meeting rooms. There is another set of treasures that are architectural—whole buildings whose form and content embody creative demonstrations of their time. The Divinity School, much battled over in recent years, has a breathtaking courtyard modeled after the Lawn of Thomas Jefferson's University of Virginia. Peeling paint and empty rooms hint at troubled times, but the Marquand Chapel, at the courtyard's head, has been fully restored, and the school's old residential rooms will soon be renovated as well. At the corner of York and Chapel is another remarkable architectural achievement—Paul Rudolph's Art and Architecture building. Rudolph designed this home for his school when he was dean, and the much-praised and -maligned build-

ing has undergone damaging alterations through its forty-year life. In our photograph of the A&A, taken from the fifth-floor walkway, looking down onto the fourth-floor studio spaces, we can see the Roman statue of Minerva overlooking the students' drawing tables. Long thought to be a late and poor copy of an original marble figure, Minerva suffered the indignity of supporting a student-installed basketball hoop for a number of years, until a horrified art historian realized that she was an original. Minerva now resides in the Yale University Art Gallery. Yale's arts area renovation promises to restore Rudolph's extraordinary building to its original glory.

135 *The organ in the Marquand Chapel of the Yale Divinity School.* **136** *Three samples of Samuel Yellin's ironwork, which adorns the residential colleges.* **137** *A view down into the fourth-floor studio area of Paul Rudolph's Art and Architecture building, photographed shortly after the building opened in 1963.*

138

The printed zebra was impressed onto paper by the very block that sits above it in this photograph made in the Arts of the Book Room at Sterling Memorial Library. Lead type and copper halftone cuts were the matrices by which most printed matter was made during the first two-thirds of the twentieth century. Yale's Arts of the Book Room records the history of this technology. It is a repository of the ephemera of the age of letterpress printing and the home to many rare volumes that exist between the incunabula of the Beinecke Library and the dog-eared working volumes of Sterling and Cross Campus libraries. For many years this collection ran on half-steam, open for only part of each day and never fully supported financially by the University. Today it has become a full-time operation, and the collection has recently added the library of Paul Rand, one of the seminal graphic designers of our time. Type and blocks have disappeared in the world outside, and the rapid and cheap technologies of photography and the computer dominate printing today, so this precious collection holds irreplaceable bits of our literary history.

139

140

141

There is a touchy aspect to public art that comes to Yale's campus. The short version of the problem is that only the very best should be allowed here, for nothing is as embarrassing as bad art that hangs around for a long time. Even with an oversight committee to review the placement of major outdoor installations, there is a risk of putting the wrong thing in the wrong place. The Oldenburg *Lipstick* is the best sort of art to have in our courtyards; it is engaging, perfectly resonant of its period, and yet lasting in its effect. The original *Lipstick* had a highly suggestive inflatable top, but this fabric component would never have survived out in the weather. The permanent sculpture, which stands in the Morse College courtyard, has a relatively innocent fiberglass tip. We can make the case that a successful installation like this one has an impact comparable to that of a tenured professor who spends a long teaching life shaping Yale. This comparison seems apt to the artists among us, though it might horrify those for whom art carries little importance.

138 Objects from the collection of the Arts of the Book Room. 139 Yale's font of Chinese lead type, more than 55,000 characters, which used to stretch all the way across the basement of the Graduate School. 140 Setting up Claes Oldenburg's Lipstick. 141 The Lipstick in its final manifestation in the courtyard of Morse College.

142 Unveiling the Vinland Map in the Beinecke Library in 1965. 143 The Genesis Fragment. Among the earliest pieces of original Christian writing, this papyrus from Egypt dates to before A.D. 100. 144 The Harkness Gutenberg Bible in its case on the mezzanine of the Beinecke Library.

The Beinecke Library is Yale's largest architectural jewel box. It sits on Hewitt Quadrangle, delicately suspended by granite pylons, so the marble-patterned facade hangs above the stone tiles of the square. Inside the Beinecke a glass-walled column of leather-bound books rises to the top of the huge single main room. Wide staircases provide access to basement reading rooms, where tables and chairs sit bathed by light reflected from white stone sculptures by Isamu Noguchi that stand in an adjacent sunken garden. Another stair takes the visitor to the mezzanine, which is a raised partial floor that wraps around the literary treasures in the central stacks. Toward the back of the mezzanine is a glass case, and there sits the Harkness Gutenberg Bible. Its two bound volumes are always open, so the viewer gets to see four of the priceless leaves of Western civilization's earliest and most beautiful printed book. Below in the storerooms are many other noteworthy Bible pages. The one reproduced opposite is thought to be the earliest extant Christian biblical fragment.

143

144

This articulated form could easily be mistaken for a new exhibit destined for the Peabody Museum. The arched back and immense front leg fit the schematic of a brontosaurus almost perfectly, and perhaps we are seeing a first attempt at filling out the frame of this prehistoric creature before it is installed in the Great Hall. The photograph actually shows the construction of the reinforced-concrete backbone of Ingalls Rink, and its apparent affinity to biological form reminds us how much architecture changed in the twentieth century.

Yale's building boom of the 1930s created a campus of archaic architectural styles, where stone, glass, and hidden steel emulated medieval building styles. Eero Saarinen's ice rink, built thirty years later, based its structure on the curves and tensions of living creatures, to the extent that the building is commonly called the Whale. This immense cement arch anchors cables that support the roof, providing skaters with a full-sized rink with sweeping interior scale and no disruptive columns.

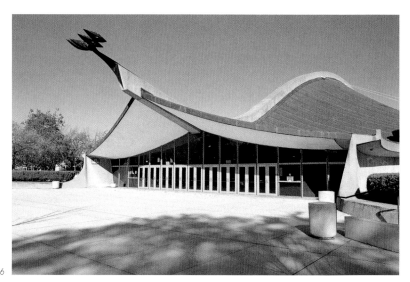

145 Ingalls Rink, under construction.   **146** The front door of the rink today.
147 A May Day meeting in Ingalls Rink in the spring of 1970, when students planned demonstrations to show their solidarity with the Black
Panthers.

148

148 Danny Kaye speaking to Kingman Brewster. Kaye was a faithful sup-
porter of the School of Music. **149** A Theater Studies production of
Dancing at Lughnasa, in the Old Lincoln Theater. **150** The cover from the
Whiffenpoofs' sixtieth-anniversary record album, produced in 1969. **151**
Communiversity Day, when administrators, faculty, students, and New
Haven politicians played a life-sized game of chess on Cross Campus.

152

153

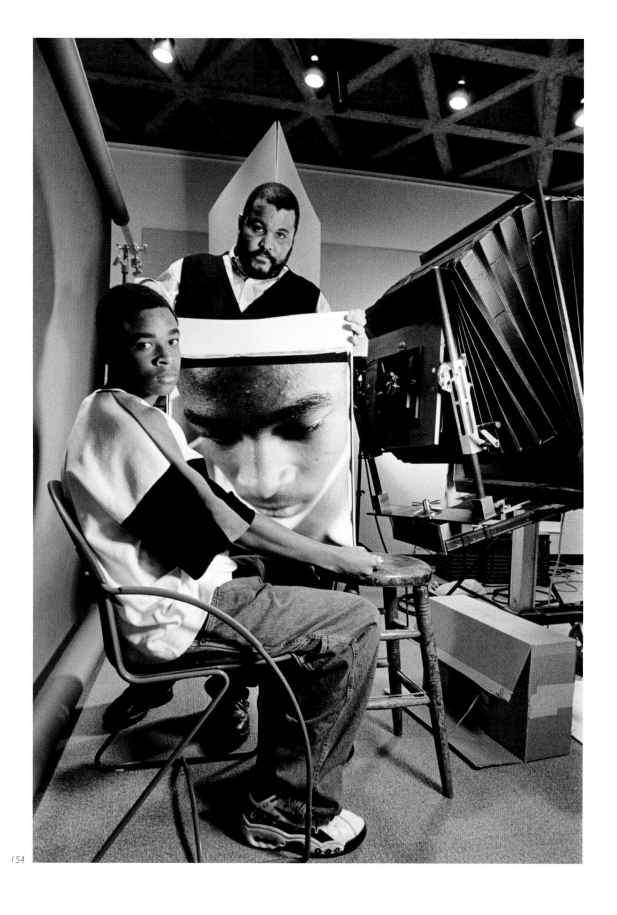

154

152 Marcel Duchamp's Revolving Glass, *happily spinning away at the Yale University Art Gallery after its recent restoration.* **153** *A color study in construction paper, by Chi Yung Chung, a graduate of the School of Art in 1998. This collage is based upon the Van Gogh painting* Night Cafe, *which hangs in the Art Gallery. Students in Professor Richard Lytle's color class make studies such as this as a way of understanding the use of colors by the great painters of the past.* **154** *Dawoud Bey, Yale MFA 1989, photographing New Haven schoolchildren for an artist-in-residence program funded by the Art Gallery.*

155 *Paul Mellon, photographed in his Yale Center for British Art, home to the finest collection of British paintings, drawings, and prints in America. This invaluable collection, amassed by Mellon through many years of diligent pursuit, is housed in the last building by the great architect Louis Kahn.* **156** *Pumpkin with a Stable-Lad, painted by George Stubbs in 1774.*

Paul Mellon was one of the supreme benefactors of Yale. He supported the arts, funded education in the residential colleges, and even backed the construction of Morse and Ezra Stiles colleges. Everywhere we look in this century we find his beneficent hand. Paul Mellon was a great figure in his person as well; sweet, immensely cultured, sensitive to others, and kind beyond description. There will never be another like him. Above is a reproduction of the first painting he bought, *Pumpkin with a Stable-Lad* by George Stubbs, which touched off Mellon's unparalleled career as a collector. In his memoirs he recounts the discovery and purchase of another painting by Stubbs, and this description reveals much about the man:

A third Stubbs came to me in a most unlikely fashion. A lady in Manitoba, Canada, wrote to me saying she had heard that I was interested in Stubbs, that she and her family had a small Stubbs painting of a leopard on Wedgwood porcelain, which they had inherited, and would I be interested? I wrote asking if she would send me a photograph. Eventually a very badly lightflashed Polaroid arrived, but even I was pretty well convinced that the picture was right. I then wrote to her asking if she would entrust it to me and to Basil [Taylor] to authenticate and whether we

might be allowed to have it cleaned by the Conservation Department of the Victoria and Albert Museum. She agreed to this and sent me the painting. Apart from being very dirty and having a crack running through it, it certainly looked Stubbish and attractive.

Basil pronounced it genuine as soon as he saw it, and the V&A did a magnificent job of restoration. I reported all this to the lady in Manitoba and inquired whether she would like to sell it to me. I suggested that I get three independent experts to appraise the work and that I would, to be more than fair, pay her the amount of the highest estimate. This appraisal turned out to be fifty thousand dollars, and the deal was consummated. We never corresponded again, and I have often wondered if she is still happy with the transaction, whether she is still in Manitoba or in heaven.

IX Life at Yale in the Eighties and Nineties

Yale University has twelve deans: ten run the professional schools, one handles the Graduate School, and one is the master of Yale College. For five years the University has had the great good fortune to have Richard Brodhead as the Dean of Yale College. One of his duties is to give the welcoming address to the incoming freshmen, and these annual speeches are among the best pieces of oratory that the University has to offer. Here is an excerpt from the address to incoming freshmen in 1997.

Freshman Address

RICHARD H. BRODHEAD

What an astonishing coincidence! My friends and I have set out for a stroll, and who should we run into but the Yale College Class of 2001! By yet more amazing chance, we had decided to try out our academic casualwear, and you too have gone in for an elegant formality! What could this massive fashion statement mean? We have put on noncustomary outfits to mark an extraordinary occasion: the formal start of a great new life. Think of it: you are released forever from the stressful and absorbing work of getting into college. No more standardized testing for you, no more essays requiring you to explain, with becoming humility, why you are the most impressive person you've ever met. More seriously, you are crossing the threshold into a space of wildly enriched possibility, a world where opportunities for discovery and self-discovery will assault you at every turn. And since you have reached the age of reason, the restrictions needful for the immature will now be very largely suspended, so that you will confront these opportunities with expanded freedom and responsibility. On this occasion, when I name the new school you have come to, I mean to indicate the new chances and powers you've come for. You will now understand me when I say (when I say it it's official, so prepare yourself for a life-altering pronouncement): Men and women of the Class of 2001, welcome to Yale College.

157

Two thousand and one is a resonant number here even without its futuristic associations. Yale College having been founded in 1701, you have the distinction of being Yale's tercentennial class, and we will celebrate Yale's three hundredth birthday together with your graduation. This fact could remind you that in entering Yale you are stepping into a long-running history. When the personal computer was born, Yale was already 280 years old. When electric power first became available and telephone networks were first established, Yale was already nearly 180. The Civil War and the Emancipation Proclamation are nearer to the present than they are to Yale's beginning. To go back to the great early landmark of the American women's movement, the Seneca Falls Convention of 1848, is to cross just half the distance between 1997 and 1701. Among more venerable rivals, Yale is older than the American nation and modern democratic government; older than the industrial revolution; older, arguably, than modern capitalism, Adam Smith's *The Wealth of Nations* having appeared so recently as 1776.

What you are coming into has been going on for a long time. But when people come here as students, whoever Yale may have belonged to before, it becomes their place—theirs to enjoy and theirs to help create. I wonder if you have any idea how much Yale is about to be in your power. Every year when we admit a class we put this place at risk. The joyous creativity of students here, their high-spirited pursuit of excellence in a thousand forms of work and play, helps make the supremely interesting world that Yale lovers love. But what if some year Yale fell into the hands of dullards and lethargiacs? This whole place could go dead. In the discussion classes that are so common here each student has the power to help co-create a deepening group awareness, to join the inquiry and lead it to unexpected turns. If some year students fell into docility or torpor, just wanted to be told the answer and go back to bed, there would be a stiff price for us: the whole activity of understanding would have been diminished. This is now your place, and it is now for you to give it life and realize its promise. My first message to you was a joyful welcome, but I follow it with a stern command: Now get to work; make this place happen.

158

Above we see staff members carrying a new rug, which will go into the President's Room on the second floor of Woolsey Hall. Those bearing the snakelike load are a mixed group. Cooks, physical plant staff, and others whose jobs are unknown all lend a hand for this tough job. Only with such cooperation could the rug make its way up the curved stairs that rise from the wings of the rotunda, to end up smoothly in place on the floor of the ornate meeting room that many never see in their time at Yale.

On the facing page is a group of administrators and faculty struggling with the task of undergraduate admissions. No job is more important than that of choosing the incoming students. Gaining admission to any top school is a challenge for students that is as daunting as any they will face in their lives. But those screening the candidates also face an immense task, sorting through the vast number of applications, paying adequate attention to each one, and then making the difficult choices that create the student body.

The faculty and students get the glory at Yale, and the resplendent President and Provost ride at the head of this ship of education, but standing behind it are huge numbers of people who labor to make the whole affair function. They type, paint, wire, cook, nail, address, calculate, pack, mail, measure, dig, pave, mow, water, serve, wash, clean, and carry out endless other tasks. They are as important to the structure of the University as our own hearts and feet are to our bodies. Our health depends upon theirs and theirs upon ours, and each would fail without the other.

Whether in a classroom, or seated by the open window of a dorm, the Yale student is constantly using printed books. In this much-touted electronic age we still receive most of our communication from the past via the printed page, and our old ally paper is more prevalent than ever. The Yale Daily News is still printed overnight, so each new day has an inky headline to shout the news. The libraries of Yale continue to grow at an astonishing rate. Electronic media are powerful tools for education, but it is hard to beat the comfort of a dog-eared old volume that can speak to us while we lean against a sunlit tree and take in the thoughts of an author who is distant in space and time.

161–162 *Studying indoors and out on the Old Campus.* **163** *A view into the Yale Daily News at night.*

161

163

This is a Yale blackboard, freshly erased at the end of class. It appears that the board was wiped with a cloth, or one of those blocky erasers that holds the white dust just long enough to lift it off the board and onto the coatsleeve of the user. The blackboard retains a record of the cleaning, and then, on top of the streaks, it bears the striking imprint of a human hand. The black-and-whiteness of slate, chalk, and person are enigmatically mingled in the narrative world of this well-made picture.

Blackboards are disappearing from the campus. Every self-respecting scientist still has one in the office, usually covered with formulae and notes that are unintelligible to outsiders, but the blackboard as a species is definitely on the way out. White boards, which can take designs in different colors and are lightweight and easy to move, have undermined the supremacy of the blackboard, and now the computer has generated its own version. The new digital whiteboard is beginning to crop up around campus, and as we build classrooms or renovate old ones, the traditional black-slate teach-ing tool will gradually disappear. Maybe the hand is also on the way out. We have always been more interested in the mind than the hand at Yale, and nowadays more and more work that used to be done with pen, pencil, or chalk is carried out by simply tapping on a computer keyboard. Someday soon we will probably just speak to our computers instead of even touching them.

165

164 A blackboard in a Yale College classroom. *165* Jonathan Spence, Sterling Professor of History, lecturing in Battell Chapel.

166

167

168

166 Bruce Ackerman, Sterling Professor of Law and Political Science, lecturing in the Law School. 167 Students in the School of Management. 168 Lamin Sanneh, D. Willis James Professor of Missions and World Christianity, teaching at the Divinity School.

169 *Aldo Parisot, Samuel S. Sanford Professor of Music, giving (and thoroughly enjoying) a cello lesson.* **170** *A solar car produced by students in mechanical engineering, on display outside the Beinecke Library.* **171** *Astronomy students at the University observatory in Bethany.*

170

There has always been a delicate truce between the hand and mind in university life. Yale has a set of ten professional schools dedicated to teaching and research that is intimately connected to the physical world, and this has allowed Yale College to concentrate on the development of the student's mind. This is a nice theory, but the practice is hard to maintain, for so much of education is accessible only through physical activity. We see this in the arts, where a substantial undergraduate population studies in the relevant professional schools, and we see it in science, where the basis of all understanding must be grounded in the experimental method. There is a long history of engineering at Yale, but efforts to create a graduate school of engineering have never succeeded. Scattered throughout the University, however, are the physical tools for research and education in the physical sciences, and so there is a rich educational opportunity at Yale for the undergraduate interested in these fields.

171

172

173

172–175 *Dorothea Hoffmann and Pat Marino leading a graduate graphic design class to the top of Harkness Tower.*

174

This view to the northwest, from the top of Harkness Tower, shows the layered campus. Saybrook College is in the foreground, then comes Trumbull, and then the huge bulk of the Sterling Memorial Library, to the right of the picture's center. Farther away is the tower of the Hall of Graduate Studies, the blocklike buildings of Saarinen's Morse and Ezra Stiles colleges, and then the looming cathedral of the Payne Whitney Gymnasium. Yale reaches up into the city of New Haven with these buildings, and they form an arc that encloses the Broadway commercial district, which we see at left center. This area, now almost entirely owned by the University, is a testing ground for Yale's ability to revitalize a part of town by being an inspired landlord.

176

177

In some ways the domestic life of Yale has remained relatively unchanged in this century. Because of the residential college system, the earlier, intimate social scale of old Yale has been preserved even as the University has grown dramatically. Cooks make pasta for thousands, blossoms are cut to decorate common room dining tables, and the Old Campus is the scene of lively freshman activity. Rooms are still packed with belongings, but the contents have changed since the days of the bicentennial. Every room has its electronic gadgets and stacks of those little mirrored disks that bring hi-fi music into what once were quiet spaces, where books and conversation used to reign unchallenged. The rooms have a disarray that would shock parents from years gone by; no maids or servants make the beds up each day, and blankets and towels are thrown about with casual disregard. The chaos we see in our children's rooms today simply reflects the speed and intensity of change that characterizes modern life. Only those born into these complex times can live comfortably in them, and all the stone walls and leaded windows of Yale cannot subdue the pace of young lives today.

182

There are endless parties at Yale, and many of them are closely linked to specific residential colleges. Saybrook has its double-courtyard bash, Pierson has the Halloween inferno—where rumor has it that a newly arrived freshman can behave in ways never allowed at home—and Morse has its Casino night. This picture of undergraduates decked out in evening clothes for a night of serious gambling was taken in 1995, but there is something a bit dated about the scene; it looks more like the excesses of the twenties than the last decade of the twentieth century.

180 Willie Ruff, professor of music, blowing his horn in Sprague Hall. 181 Shawn Colvin at a Master's Tea at Silliman College. Seated with her is Kelly Brownell, professor of psychology and epidemiology and public health, who is the Master of Silliman. 182 Casino night at Morse College.

135

183

The bladderball varied between six and eight feet in diameter, depending on how vigorously it was being shoved around by students. The object of the University-wide mayhem that ensued when bladderball was played was to bring the ball to one's own residential college, or some other assigned goal. Hordes of undergraduates gathered beneath the ball and hit it up into the air. The crowd followed the bouncing sphere, even as it moved through courtyards and gateways into New Haven streets. Everyone had a taste of exciting mob frenzy, but the whole endeavor was just too hazardous to exist in our sanitized modern lifestyle. Since the end of the bladderball era, things haven't been quite the same.

184

183 *In a pose that would strike terror in the hearts of any parent—or Yale administrator—two undergraduates perch on the gutter of Lawrence Hall, four floors up, beer in hand, and watch the bladderball antics below.* **184** *Bladderball in full swing on the Old Campus.*

185

186

187

188

185 *Maya Lin's* Women's Table, *on the Rose Walk in front of Sterling Memorial Library.* **186** *A large fiberglass salmon, posed outside Sterling to raise campus awareness of the plight of the salmon.* **187** *Two Yale College students working for Habitat for Humanity on a public-service project sponsored by Dwight Hall.* **188** *A young postdoctoral fellow visiting the Medical School.*

When students come to Yale, their lives are turned upside down in magical and irreversible ways. This partly occurs because the age at which we attend college is one of the most impressionable times in our lives, but change also comes because a freshman is thrust into a population unlike any previously experienced. Students find themselves in a community of peers who share the intelligence and inquisitiveness that often was a social handicap in their earlier lives. Every one of them is interesting and interested, and the first days at Yale hold a revelation of newfound friends and colleagues.

When the campus population was white and male, the same principles applied, but we can now look back on these earlier times and see how insular the communal population of the College was. Now Yale is a stage for students from all parts of the world, male and female, rich and poor, black and white, western and eastern. The University is dedicated to the belief that we are one family, living in a challenging yet rewarding world. Yale's working premise is that the betterment of all life depends upon the union of the broad spectrum of human genes and the deep influences of traditional education.

A Remarkable Gathering

ALISON R. RICHARD
Provost

Asked about the challenges facing Yale in the years ahead, I travel in my mind across the landscape of the University in search of my reply. First, of course, there are the people, the need to attract the best faculty, students, and staff. Then there are the buildings, the task of returning some to splendor, replacing others, and adding still others for new purposes. I see the life of the University and the life of New Haven becoming more closely interwoven. My topic takes in all these matters, and something else entirely.

Yale is not just a remarkable gathering of people in a remarkable place, set in the midst of an increasingly lively city. It is also a community—or, perhaps more accurately, a community comprising smaller communities. From time to time, I am told that the Yale community is not what it once was. From time to time, I am told that the warmth and vibrancy of the Yale community are among its special appeals. Undergraduates don't seem to lack for community, and efforts to build a greater sense of community for graduate students are bringing about real changes for the better. We may argue about how to define the Yale community, or about its health, but I no longer have any doubts as to its reality or its importance.

I worry most about the future of the community of faculty. Let me give two illustrations, one humble and one less so, of the essence of this community. First, just walk across the campus at any time of any day, and eavesdrop on the greetings and brief collegial conversations between faculty on their way from one place to another. My second illustration builds on the first. I have stood in awe on the sidelines of many faculty recruitments over the past six years, watching the Yale faculty in action. Salary, benefits, a magnificent library, refurbished facilities, and all the good things the University can do are necessary, but rarely sufficient. The brilliance of faculty and students, the extraordinary resources of the University—these inducements carry a recruitment closer, sometimes all the way to success. But often the deal is not sealed until recruitment moves into another gear—when the life of the mind meets the life of the human being, around a dinner table, on a walk in East Rock Park, during the interval between acts at a play. These are moments of fellowship, exploration, and enjoyment. These are powerful renderings of community.

The University community is under assault today. The assault, curiously, is driven by changes many of which I welcome and applaud. The problem, the challenge, is how to protect and nurture this intangible yet indispensible feature of the University even as we welcome at least some of the changes that threaten it.

Arguably the single most crucial change is demographic. In days gone by, families lived in New Haven. Husbands were members of the Yale faculty, and wives were homemakers. The expectations with respect to the roles of men and women were quite different. Today, a two-career household with young children to raise may have little time for the kinds of activities that once served as the glue holding the community together. For many couples with positions in different cities, living some distance from the campus has become a necessity.

The past fifty years have brought an explosion of knowledge, particularly in the sciences, and this explosion has been accompanied by increased specialization. For students, there is simply more to learn about a particular subject, and this demand for concentration puts at risk the breadth of their education; faculty members, in turn, are drawn to identify more with their academic subdiscipline than with the intellectual community of the University. Intolerance lurks in the shadows of ignorance of other modes of inquiry, and epistemological divisions threaten the health both of single disciplines and of the community as a whole.

The advent of the Internet is held out as an innovation whose impact will be as profound as that of the invention of the printing press. This is not yet evident in higher education, but Yale must be in the vanguard of this movement. These technologies can reshape the ways teaching and learning take place, and they will require us to articulate more clearly than ever why it is worth coming to a particular place called Yale to be educated. At the same time, these technologies will enable us to reach out to other kinds of students. There will be risks as well as opportunities in this vision of a worldwide virtual classroom. More prosaically, for the time being it makes it easier for faculty to work from home instead of in their offices.

With the good fortune to have professional schools as part of the heart and soul of the institution, Yale has long had one foot outside the Ivory Tower. It is all the more curious, then, that the University has been a relative latecomer to the developing world of relations with the corporate world. Such partnerships bring many benefits, including research support, student internships, and "start-up" business ventures for faculty and students alike, as well as the less tangible benefits that flow from connecting the academy to other kinds of endeavors. These connections are springing up in many parts of the University, bringing new ideas and opportunities in their wake. But here too, there are shoals upon which the ship of the community may founder as more and more time and energy are diverted away from it.

If these are some of the sources of the challenge, what should our response be? Turn the clock back, ignore the changes, or lament the passing of a Golden Age? In my view, that would be variously ineffective, wrong, or foolish. With the single exception of the trend toward balkanization of scholarship and education, which needs to be confronted and wrestled with on its own terms, the other changes of which I write are integral features of a great university today. What, then, can we do?

Most important by far, I believe, is to recognize and celebrate Yale's sense of community—to make vigilance on its behalf a state of mind informing all that we do. Such a state of mind can inform the way in which spaces are refurbished or new facilities laid out. It can launch new academic programs. It can focus new attention on ways in which the residential colleges—Yale's most essential communities—might embrace other parts of the University. It can help guide the University's policies concerning conflicts of commitment. It can be a touchstone as we navigate our way into e-space. It can be . . . and it already is. Evidence abounds of efforts to reaffirm and nurture Yale's sense of community. The challenge is to keep working at it, hard.

189

189 *The gutted interior of Connecticut Hall, Yale's oldest and most illustrious building, during its complete renovation in 1953.* 190 *Berkeley College during its 1998 restoration.*

The sad truth is that the treasures of the past wear out and disappear unless we take care of them. Any institution needs to preserve its physical objects, Yale has a maintenance task of immense proportions. Some things wear out through use, like the steps into Woolsey Hall, which have the rounded edges shaped by a hundred years of foot traffic. Others disintegrate because their materials cannot hold up to the passages of time and weather, which steadily erode all things. Yale's buildings also suffer from the incessantly changing populations that inhabit them, and so residences and classrooms must be continually rebuilt if they are to stay with us. Pieces of art, whether paintings or books and manuscripts, are destroyed by more subtle means, as humidity and internal chemical imbalance slowly alter their original appearance. One challenge facing the University in the new century is to preserve what we have, but we also must be careful to create new assets that will ease the burden on conservators of the future.

190

191 Leather bindings and paper signatures under the attack of their own internal acidity. 192 Books in Sterling Memorial Library awaiting preservation.

The first printed books were made of rag paper, using the recycled fibers of cotton cloth. Because of their permanence we have astounding artifacts from the past, like the Beinecke Library's Harkness Gutenberg Bible, which is as sturdy and legible as on the day it was finished. In the nineteenth century, when the world population grew, and with it the demand for books, wood pulp began to be used for papermaking. This new paper turned acidic with time, and books made from it crumbled to the touch after a few decades. We face the irony that printed records of relatively modern times are disappearing while earlier volumes last beautifully. Nowadays paper manufacturers use different chemistry in their papers, so today's books should be around for quite a while. Yale, which has collected books throughout its long life, faces a nearly insuperable problem in preserving the acid-paper volumes of the past century.

One of the treasures shared by Yale and New Haven is Hillhouse Avenue. This glorious street, two blocks between Grove and Sachem, is owned by the city but is lined with buildings that are almost all owned by Yale. Many of these historic buildings are superb examples of the architecture of the nineteenth century, and they originally housed wealthy families and members of the Yale community. The fortunes of the industrial revolution were the means by which these beautiful houses were built, and so as coal, steam, and rampant manufacture made a mess of the landscape, Hillhouse became a showplace of the era's lovelier side. Yale must carefully balance preservation of the street with the University's need to educate in suitable spaces, and so, as these buildings have been restored, their interiors have been carefully converted into administrative and teaching rooms. Perhaps the most beautiful of all the buildings there is 46 Hillhouse, which has been renovated to join others at the Sachem end of the street as part of the School of Management. How appropriate that the business leaders of the future will be educated in the creations of an earlier period of fabulous financial growth.

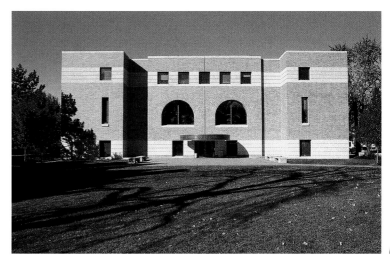

196

When the University builds new facilities, it faces a tough choice: either eliminate something old or expand in size. The issue seems illogical to those who want the innovation, but the delicate balance between the new, the old, and the status quo must always be in the forefront of the administration's planning. There are always parts of Yale that need improvement, and the marvelous new Music Library is an elegant example of how such a need can be addressed. By enclosing a courtyard in Sterling Memorial Library and building a state-of-the-art music facility, Yale has created a new educational space within the existing footprint of the library. The Irving S. Gilmore Music Library has been added to Yale, but an old open space has been given up in exchange.

The need to exercise caution as we preserve the old, eliminate the obsolete, and add the new holds as a principle on every level of our University. We must not add programs unless we cut others or make a carefully examined decision to grow larger; we shouldn't even accept the gift of something as delectable as a new artwork for one of the museums unless we understand the ramifications in housing, conservation, and preservation that will be assumed for the indefinite future of Yale's collections. Making these decisions often puts the University administration in touchy positions, but the ongoing success of our educational enterprise depends on such discrimination.

193 The Trowbridge house, 46 Hillhouse Avenue, the last private building on Hillhouse to become part of the University. This building has now been brilliantly restored, and it serves as the International Center for Finance, under the direction of the School of Management. 194 A view south down Hillhouse Avenue. 195 Henry R. Luce Hall, 34 Hillhouse Avenue, completed in 1995. Because the architectural style of this building is different from the other Hillhouse Avenue homes, it has been set farther back on its lot to preserve the visual integrity of the street. 196 The new Irving S. Gilmore Music Library. Built in 1998, this library, fully equipped for the study of books, manuscripts, and recordings, was created by enclosing a large open courtyard that was landlocked within the walls of the Sterling Memorial Library.

All living things need to adapt to changing conditions, and the continuing life of the University is dependent upon its ability to accommodate changing times. Today the development of digital educational tools is testing Yale's resiliency. The card catalog of Sterling Memorial Library, housed on the first floor, is one of the wonders of the campus. For more than one hundred years paper cards have listed and cross-referenced the holdings of the University's libraries. In alcove after alcove wait stools and study tables, pencils and scratch paper, oak drawers stuffed with index cards. In the past dozen years this system has been upended by the introduction of computer-manipulated databases applied to library cataloging. Now the cool stone corners of Sterling's catalog floor house the immensely powerful screens of Orbis, Yale's electronic library card catalog. There is still much information in the cards that is not yet on the hard drives, but the speed of Orbis—along with its inherent suitability to the digitally trained minds of young people—means that the old index cards will disappear within a few years.

198

The computer made its place in the library gradually, but it entered the arts at Yale with a bang in the fall of 1998. In September the Digital Media Center for the Arts was opened at 149 York Street, the old home of the Yale Printing Service. It is a nice irony that digital machines have turned up on the very floors where ink-based presses used to dispense University information.

The DMCA was created to provide a venue for students and faculty to work collaboratively with the new computer technologies. Each of the art-related institutions at Yale faces a computer crisis because the cost of installing and maintaining these machines is beyond its individual budgetary capacities. This challenge, coupled with the cross-disciplinary nature of the digital world, led to the creation of the DMCA. At the center are PCs and Macs, digital video cameras and editing stations, and the vital staff needed to keep them all running. The center is an interim facility, destined to grow into Yale's own particular response to the possibilities of students, pixels, and creative energy in the twenty-first century.

197 *Computers set up in a card catalog alcove on the first floor of the Sterling Memorial Library.* **198** *Students at a video editing workstation in the Digital Media Center for the Arts.*

XI Commencement

199

If we looked down from the sky onto a Yale Commencement, it would be a mystifying spectacle. Hordes of adults march in groups, wearing flowing black robes and funny square hats, and skinny blue folders are passed out to joyous applause. Vendors sell hot dogs and balloons on city streets that have been blocked off to traffic, and people of every stripe gather in tight groups to watch this bizarre spectacle. It is a medieval event transported to the present, with modern sensibilities dictating that a glorious party take place concurrent with the serious ceremony of graduation. Newly degreed young folks pass through a watershed in their lives and embark on varied careers. Thousands of parents sigh with relief as they witness the final stage of the educations they have been paying for over the years. Little do the graduates know how persistently their friends from Yale will stick through the next decades of their lives, or how often the recollection of a meaningful classroom moment will come to rescue them in some intel-

lectually demanding moment in the future. One thing is sure: no one is the same after being a student at Yale, and as the years tick by, this life-altering period will continue to exert its power.

199 *A vendor selling balloons on Elm Street during a Commencement in the 1940s.* **200** *The academic procession snaking its way past the Ledyard Flagstaff on Hewitt Quadrangle. This photograph, from the late forties, was taken before the construction of the Beinecke Library. The trees in the center background are in the approximate location now occupied by the Beinecke.*

201

Yale gives degrees in many areas of study, and at various levels of advancement. There are bachelor's degrees in arts or sciences, and master's degrees and doctorates offered by the Graduate School or the professional schools. Degrees can also be divided into categories according to how they have been earned.

First is the degree awarded for the completion of a particular course of study. These are the ones granted at Commencement to those at Yale who have accumulated the necessary earned credits. Next comes the "privatim" degrees, which are awarded by the University to senior faculty who don't have a degree from Yale or some comparable institution. This rather odd honor seems to exist to reinforce the University's sense of being a single family, to enrich the credentials of the faculty, and (some say) to create additional

affluent alumni for the ever-waiting hands of the fund-raisers. Finally, honorary degrees awarded by Yale to a small number of great achievers, including some who have worked outside academic circles, whose work has had a significant impact on the world at large. These honorands always attend Commencement, and their association with the University brings a mutual sense of pride. The list of honorands is a closely guarded secret each year. They don their robes in the Corporation Room at Woodbridge Hall, then walk to Old Campus at the head of the academic procession, as onlookers crane their necks to see what great people will be on the platform this year.

202

201 *President Franklin D. Roosevelt, at Yale to receive an honorary degree in 1934. He is supported by President Angell of Yale on the left and President Conant of Harvard on the right.* **202** *Duke Ellington, in the Corporation Room in Woodbridge Hall, putting on his robes before receiving his honorary degree in 1967.*

203

204

205

206

203 Some music for the start of the festivities. 204 Yale College Associate Dean John Meeske, ready to lead the students into the Old Campus. 205 A graduate of the School of Music—no doubt an opera major—decked out in Brünnhilde's helmet. 206 Georges May, center, discussing the workings of the academic world with Richard Levin, then Dean of the Graduate School, left, and Jaroslav Pelikan, Sterling Professor of History. 207 A graduating senior decked out in garlands for the occasion.

207

208

208 President Howard Lamar, leading the academic procession in 1993.
209 The physicist Stephen Hawking, on his way to the Old Campus,
where he received an honorary degree in 1993. **210** Crossing Elm
Street, the procession moves from Cross Campus to the Old Campus.

209

Commencement usually takes place on a brilliant spring day, when the breeze blows fresh off Long Island Sound and the newly opened leaves wear that elusive yellow-green that precedes the heavy colors of summer. Hordes of spectators come to see the graduation—friends and families of the students, alumni who can't bear to miss the event, and countless others who line the streets and sidewalks. Seats are assigned for faculty, students, and ticket-holding guests, but so many attend that every possible perch becomes a seat. The steps of Wright Hall, the bases of lampposts, and the fences on the Old Campus all sprout people, straining to see above the crowd.

211 Commencement guests seated on the steps of Dwight Hall, on the Old Campus. **212** Family and friends of the graduates enjoying Commencement on a beautiful day, beneath the green trees of the Old Campus and the looming backdrop of Harkness Tower.

Yale's graduation ceremonies ignore the weather, and the degree candidates, faculty, and guests all sit out under the open sky; the only exceptions are the honorands, the Yale Corporation Fellows, and the University leaders, who have the benefit of a blue-and-white-striped tent above their heads. Once in a while rain falls on Commencement, and the crowd becomes a textured field of umbrellas. On rare occasions the weather is so bad that the ceremonies must be shortened. The normal practice of having the deans announce their respective candidates is shelved, and the President salutes the whole group in one simple statement. But even then the honorary degree candidates are properly inducted, one at a time.

214

Robert Frank made this photograph of a Yale graduation in 1955, while he was on a Guggenheim Fellowship. The picture appears in *The Americans,* Frank's influential book published in 1956 with an accompanying text by Jack Kerouac. Robert Frank has always been the purest of artists, and he has produced remarkable work in photography, film, and collage. He disdains worldly goods and lives a spartan life with his wife, the sculptor June Leaf. Each has an ongoing history of producing innovative and important work.

In the 1950s Frank befriended a Chinese painter named Sanyu, who was living in poverty in New York City. Robert purchased some of Sanyu's paintings, at a time when neither of them had any money to speak of. In the mid-1990s, long after Sanyu's death, these pictures were sold. Funds from the sale of Sanyu's work went to the Andrea Frank Foundation, named for Robert's daughter, and in 1998 this foundation gave $500,000 to the Yale School of Art to create the Sanyu Scholarship Fund for tuition support for students from China.

215

Josef Albers, Doctor of Fine Arts, 1962

Professor Emeritus of Art, Yale University. Yale pays homage
to you as teacher, artist, and poet. You have demonstrated in
your work the truth uttered in Plato's *Philebus* when
Socrates said, "I assert that the beauty of the straight line
and the circle and the plane . . . is not relative like that of
other things, but that they are always absolutely beautiful."
While dedicated to your own style, you have nonetheless
maintained in your teaching a universal point of view recog-
nizing the values inherent in the great art of all ages. Mind-
ful of your contributions in a decade of leadership in its
School of Art and Architecture, Yale confers upon you the
degree of Doctor of Fine Arts.

216

Artur Rubinstein, Doctor of Music, 1962

Master of the pianoforte, you have re-created the classics of your art with vitality and impeccable taste. Today, well into the second half-century of an international career, you continue to astonish the world by the vigor and freshness of your interpretations and by the monumental design of your programs. An aristocrat of the concert stage, you manifest in your person the elegance of those noblemen among composers whose works you instinctively choose to perform. In the conviction that Parnassus crowns the interpretive artist as well as the composer, Yale confers upon you the degree of Doctor of Music.

215 *President Griswold awarding an honorary degree to Josef Albers in 1962. Albers led the School of Art from 1951 to 1959, when it encompassed the fields of art, architecture, and design. In the foreground sits Artur Rubinstein, who also received an honorary degree that year.* **216** *The faculty, enjoying their Commencement seats just in front of the viewing stand.* **217** *Graduates from the School of Nursing, gleefully throwing Band-Aids in the air as their degrees are announced.*

220

218 Kingman Brewster, working the crowd during a Commencement.
219 A. Bartlett Giamatti, giving some advice to Benno Schmidt at the
latter's inauguration ceremony, 1986. ***220*** *A scene in the Yale University*
Art Gallery's Weir Courtyard, where a Henry Moore sculpture overlooks
the debris of a School of Art graduation ceremony.

Kingman Brewster is gone, and so is Bart Giamatti. Benno Schmidt ran the University for a few years, and then he went on to other things. Each year there comes a time when the crowds, too, are gone, and the grand party of Commencement is over. This is only right: all parties are short-lived, for they derive their meaning from the celebration of other, more serious times. The daily work of faculty and students at Yale consists of much drudgery interspersed with moments of revelation. We all need to let loose and boogie at times, and the academic year is packed with little events that keep everyone going. Still, the pressure builds until Commencement finally arrives, when those who graduate can say good-bye in one great burst of celebration. Afterward the empty seats and littered grass mark this ending for the students, but to those who live and work at Yale all these events are a recurring part of the University's life.

163

221

Entering Yale's Fourth Century

PRESIDENT RICHARD C. LEVIN

October 26, 1996

We enter Yale's fourth century with a firm foundation and a clear direction. We reaffirm those values that have made Yale distinctive among the world's great universities—a commitment to undergraduate education and a determination to educate leaders. We have unique excellence in the humanities and the arts, and we have the capacity to sustain it. We stand among the world's best in the biological sciences and medicine, and we are prepared to maintain our position despite near-term threats of diminished external support. We intend to sustain and enhance excellence in all our academic endeavors, selectively, as our resources permit. And to achieve that excellence, we will draw strength from the interconnectedness of this place, from a whole that is greater than the sum of its parts, a single university.

Like our predecessors a hundred years ago, we have highly imperfect foresight. We cannot say what Yale will be in fifty or one hundred years, but our strategy for the first decade or two is clear enough. To maintain Yale's distinctive strengths, we will invest, on a scale not seen since the 1930s, in the renewal of our residential colleges and libraries, as well as our athletic, arts, and science facilities. We will move aggressively to reap the fruits of the new information technologies in our teaching, research, and communication. We will build our competency in those areas of teaching and research that will assume increasing importance in the foreseeable future—such as international and environmental studies. Indeed, we will continue the transformation of Yale, begun in the eighteenth century, from a local to a regional to a national and now to a truly international institution—international in the composition of its faculty and student body as well as in the objects of its study.

We have thought hard about how to marshal the means to realize our present aspirations, and I believe that we have the financial and organizational capacity to succeed. But we need also to be flexible and adaptive. We are engaged in the generation of new knowledge, and this core activity will inevitably produce new opportunities for as yet unimagined innovations in education and research. Thus, we can have no rigid long-term plan. Instead, there must be a broad consensus on values, a shared sense of direction, and a perpetual willingness to revise yesterday's plans on the basis of new knowledge. In this spirit, we enter Yale's fourth century with confidence and commitment.

Acknowledgments

This book is the result of an indiscretion on my part. At a pleasant lunch in 1998, at the President's house, I made an ill-considered comment to the effect that a book of pictures could be put together for Yale's tercentennial that would show something of the University's rich and influential recent past. A note came to me a few days later asking whether I would be willing to assemble such a volume; still not thinking too clearly, I agreed.

Because I am a relative newcomer to Yale, having taught here only since 1979, and because I have not had the benefit of a Yale education, I doubted my qualifications to create this book. On the other hand, I have spent a lifetime with pictures, and have come to loathe the normal coffee-table book that portrays its subject with such predictability. The tercentennial deserved better, and I had assumed the responsibility of seeing to that. Yale's archives were bound to hold photographic treasures from the past one hundred years, and photographers still active today doubtless had made pictures on the fringes of their assignments that could show what the University was genuinely made of.

In preliminary discussions for the book I received great advice from Linda Lorimer, secretary of the University, and Janet Lindner, the director of tercentennial operations for Yale. These two wise friends assembled a committee for me, one whose members possess an astonishing body of knowledge about Yale; the hard work this group has applied to the project, both in dispensing knowledge about our school and in educating the book's relatively ignorant author, made this book possible. This committee, under the overall direction of Linda and Janet, but responding to my developing ideas about the book, consisted of Marie Borroff, Henry Broude, Rad Daly, Thomas Duffy, Penelope Laurans, Georges May, Judy Metro, John Ryden, Judith Schiff, and Harry Wasserman. It has been a great pleasure to meet and spend time with each of these dedicated members of the Yale community.

The photographers whose work appears here are often anonymous, and their unsigned pictures usually were found in boxes of folders in the Department of Manuscripts and Archives in the Sterling Library. I received invaluable help from Kirsten Jensen, who not only fulfilled my endless requests but also had previously found many of the best historical photographs that appear here. In the same way Geoff Zonder helped me in the archives of the Payne Whitney Gymnasium, pulling out picture after picture from a room full of file drawers. The two active photographers who contributed most to the book are Michael Marsland, of the Yale Department of Public Affairs, and Robert Lisak, a freelance photographer who graduated from the Yale School of Art in 1980. Both these men put great effort into finding the missing pieces of the book that were essential for the later years.

On the publishing front, Judy Metro, Mary Mayer, and Dan Heaton of Yale University Press skillfully guided the editing and production of the book, and John Gambell, University Printer, tuned my often rough design. Judith Schiff, Sam Chauncey, and Georges May read early drafts of the text and kindly saved me from numerous gaffes; if errors remain, it is certainly no doing of theirs. Many others, too numerous to name, had essential roles in bringing this book to completion, and I thank them all for these efforts.

Alison Richard and Jules Prown took time from hectic schedules to write essays, and Barbara Shanley and Stacey Gemmill, in the offices of the School of Art, kept me supplied with material and advice that knitted the book together. My dear wife Barbara Benson—used to it by now—listened to my constant grumbling about the project and steered me back on track when I rehearsed new and misguided notions along the way.

As a final note, let me point out that this book cannot hope to cover all the events, personalities, and developments in Yale's history for the past century. Vital people are missing, like James Rowland Angell, thought by many to have been Yale's greatest president. Pivotal events, like the alumni takeover of the curriculum in the early years of the century, are not treated. Although much is left out, I have tried to put a lot in, always bearing in mind that this book has been made for the alumni of Yale, to stir memories of their wonderful years at this grand old institution in New Haven.

Richard Benson

Photography Credits

Charles Altschul   9, 172–175, 183, 184

Erica Baum   164

Beinecke Rare Book Library   143

Richard Benson   8, 31, 37–39, 54, 97, 130–132, 134, 144, 146, 193–197

Joel Black and Jenny Fjell (courtesy of Stephen G. Waxman, M.D.)   80

Lois Conner   161, 216

Robert Frank (courtesy of Pace MacGill Gallery)   214

Courtesy of Stacey Gemmill   21, 22

Courtesy of Richard Nash Gould   150

Gail Albert Halaban   182

Courtesy of Peter Kindlmann   83

Prem Krishnamurthy   177

Courtesy of Penelope Laurans   85

Courtesy of Rick Levin   102

Robert Lisak   135, 136, 157, 158, 163, 165–169, 188, 203–213, 220

Courtesy of Richard Lytle   153

Michael Marsland   32, 87, 106, 128, 133, 138, 141, 149, 151, 154, 155, 159, 160, 162, 170, 171, 176, 178–181, 185–187, 190–192, 198, 217, 218, 221, 222

Meyers Studio (courtesy of Max Marmor)   137

New Haven Register (courtesy of Russell Goddard)   219

Archives of the Payne Whitney Gymnasium   88–90, 92–93, 95–96, 98–101, 103–105, 126, 127

Courtesy of Regina Starolis   53, 117

Garry Trudeau   94

Courtesy of Harry Wasserman   84, 129

Courtesy of Stephen G. Waxman, M.D.   79

Yale Center for British Art   156

Yale School of Medicine   16, 123

Yale School of Music   148

Yale University Art Gallery   1

Yale University Art Gallery (Joseph Szaszfai)   152

Yale University Manuscripts and Archives   2–7, 10–15, 17–20, 23–30, 33–36, 40–52, 55–78, 81–82, 86, 91, 107–116, 118–122, 124, 125, 139, 140, 142, 145, 147, 189, 199–202, 215